Derek Tangye was educated at Harrow and subsequently worked as a journalist on national newspapers. During the war and afterwards he was a member of MI5, before he and Jeannie moved to Minack. In addition to the bestselling Minack Chronicles from which the passages in this book have been selected, he was the author of *Time Was Mine*, a travel book, and *One King*, a survey of the British Commonwealth, and editor of *Went the Day Well*, a collection of tributes to those killed during the Second World War. Derek Tangye died in 1997.

Jean Nicol Tangye was the author of *Meet Me at the Savoy* and the trilogy *Hotel Regina*, *Home is the Hotel* and *Bertioni's Hotel*.

Also by Derek Tangye:

A GULL ON THE ROOF
A CAT IN THE WINDOW
A DRAKE AT THE DOOR
A DONKEY IN THE MEADOW
LAMA
THE WAY TO MINACK
A CORNISH SUMMER
COTTAGE ON A CLIFF
A CAT AFFAIR
SUN ON THE LINTEL
SOMEWHERE A CAT IS WAITING
THE WINDING LANE
WHEN THE WINDS BLOW
THE AMBROSE ROCK
A QUIET YEAR
THE CHERRY TREE
JEANNIE
GREAT MINACK STORIES
THE EVENING GULL
MONTY'S LEAP
THE STORY OF THE MINACK CHRONICLES
THE CONFUSION ROOM

Derek Tangye

THE WORLD OF MINACK

A Place for Solitude

WARNER BOOKS

A *Warner* Book

First published in Great Britain in 1991 by Michael Joseph Ltd
This edition published in 1993 by Warner Books
Reprinted 1997

A CIP catalogue record for this book
is available from the British Library.

ISBN 0 7515 0431 9

Phototypeset by Intype, London
Printed in England by Clays Ltd, St Ives plc

Warner Books
A Division of
Little, Brown and Company (UK)
Brettenham House
Lancaster Place
London WC2E 7EN

Contents

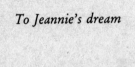

To Jeannie's dream

Introduction

The World of Minack is a form of diary. It tells the story of our life at Minack from the beginning. Many of the passages have been chosen by readers of the Minack Chronicles.

Jeannie had a passion for Minack like that of Scarlett O'Hara of *Gone with the Wind* for Tara. Minack was an obsession. She believed it belonged to those needing solitude and time for contemplation, to the birds, to the insects, the grass, the wild flowers, the animals, the bracken, the rocks, and to those of any age who yearn to be free of the conventional environment in which they are trapped . . . and she had this dream that we might find a way to keep Minack undisturbed for posterity, not just for those who might come here, but for the imagination of those who will never be able to come here.

The World of Minack echoes the reason for this dream. Will the dream become a reality?

There has been a beginning. Minack cottage, which

is rented from the estate of an old and distinguished Cornish family, has been Listed Grade II by the Department of the Environment because of the Minack Chronicles; and because of its seventeenth-century antiquity. It is now part of the English Heritage.

The Minack Chronicles Nature Trust, meanwhile, has been formed to take care of the twenty acres on the other side of the shallow valley which, as I tell in *The Ambrose Rock*, we were lucky to buy. There are four Trustees, and there are Associate Trustees, several of whom live overseas. They feel, each of them, that Minack has meant something special to them, and that they will do everything they can to preserve it, just as I am trying to do. But they will have to be on guard, as I am on guard. There will always be those who are ready to pounce on tranquillity. There will always be those intent on mutilating nature. There will always be those who are blind to beauty.

Whatever may happen, *The World of Minack* will remain a sanctuary in words, of the time Jeannie and I spent together on this wild stretch of the Cornish coast.

A Gull on the Roof

The blessing of enthusiasm is its ability to deceive pleasantly.

I sat down in our house overlooking the Thames at Mortlake and felt a soft, caressing rub at my ankle. Monty was saying in his feline fashion that he sympathised with me over the apprehension that was in my mind.

An animal, as one grows older, plays the role of the teddy bear in childhood. He stirs those qualities which are best in one's character and is one's patient confessor in periods of distress. So it was with Monty. He was, for both Jeannie and myself, the repository of our secret thoughts.

Jeannie's position was the epitome of a career girl's ambition, but it was because she was not career minded that she performed her duties so well. As public relations officer of the Savoy, Claridge's, Berkeley and Simpsons, she had a high salary, a large expense account and a multitude of friends. Her salient task had been to promote goodwill, and that was achieved not only by organising efficiently the daily routine of an office, but also by endearing herself to the great variety of people who pass through an international hotel.

My apprehension that evening was in reality an ally of the caution I had discarded; for in the morning we had set in motion our decision to leave London in favour of the bath-less, paraffin-lit, two-bedroomed cottage called Minack, and six acres of uncultivated land on the coast between Penzance and Land's End. I had completed the settlement of my own affairs and Jeannie had handed in her resignation to the Chairman of the Savoy Hotel. Our livelihood now depended upon the creation of a flower farm from this desolate, beautiful country, aided not by any practical experience but only by our ignorance as to what lay ahead.

'Absolute nonsense!' said the Chairman when Jeannie saw him, 'you're obviously tired and want a rest. Take six months holiday with pay' . . . then added: 'When you come back you will want to stay with us for ever.'

I could understand his scepticism for he had no knowledge of the months of reasoning which had brought us to this moment. He could only comprehend the fact she was throwing away a career of distinction in favour of a wild adventure which, after a short while, might appear as a misplaced enthusiasm.

He could not be expected to appreciate the sense of futility which perforce invades the kind of life we had been leading. The glamour and hospitality act as a narcotic, doping the finer instincts of living, and in the grey hours of early morning you lie awake painfully aware that you live in a flashy world where truth and integrity for the most part are despised, where slickness reigns supreme.

We found the pace too fast and any material rewards poor substitutes for the peace of mind which was sacrificed. The world of politics, journalism and entertainment in which we moved requires a ruthless zest for professional survival if you are to do so, and this neither of us now possessed. It is a world in which you cannot live on prestige alone for it is only the present that counts. We had come to distrust both the importance of the objectives and the methods used to achieve them; for it is a world in which acclaim, however transitory and gained at whatever moral cost, is valued in the same currency as the conquest of Everest.

There was no decisive occasion when we decided to leave. It was a host of occasions mingled into one, so that one day we suddenly realised our life was a spinning top, dizzily circling on one spot. We saw our fate, if we remained, in the men and women around us who had taken no heed of the barrier between youth and middle age, braying prejudiced views, dependent on the values that toppled upside down, propping against a future which repeats endlessly the present, resembling worn playing cards. We could either drift on, or start again. We could either suffer the illusion our life was a contented one and remain within the environment we knew too well, or seek freedom in a strange one.

We had been playing the game of looking for somewhere to settle whenever we had taken our holidays in Cornwall. We wanted a cottage with a wood near by and fields that went down to the sea, distant from any other habitation and remote from a countrified imitation of the life we were wishing to leave. Somewhere where we could earn a living and yet relish the isolation of a South Sea island, be able to think without being told what to think, have the leisure to study the past and live the present without interference.

It is a game which is perfectly harmless so long as no place you see fits your ideal. Once the two coincide, the moment of decision arrives and it is no longer a game. This is what happened when Jeannie and I found Minack.

The path we walked along was only a shadow of a path, more like the trodden run of badgers. Here, because there was no sign of habitation, because the land and the boulders and the rocks embraced the sea without interference, we could sense we were part of the beginning of time, the centuries of unceasing waves, the unseen pattern of the wild generations of foxes and badgers, the ageless gales that had lashed the desolate land, exultant and roaring, a giant harbour of sunken ships in their wake. And we came to a point, after a

steep climb, where a great Carn
stood balanced on a smaller one,
upright like a huge man standing
on a stool, as if it were a sentinel
waiting to hail the ghosts of lost
sailors. The track, on the other
side, had tired of the undergrowth which blocked its way
along the head of the cliff, for it
sheered seawards tumbling in a

zigzag course to the scarred grey rocks below. We stood
on the pinnacle . . . the curve of Mount's Bay leading
to the Lizard Point on the left, the Wolf Rock lighthouse
a speck in the distance, a French crabber a mile offshore,
pale blue hull and small green sail aft, chugging through
the white speckled sea towards Newlyn, and high above
us a buzzard, its wings spread motionless, soaring effortlessly into the sky.

Jeannie suddenly pointed inland. 'Look!' she said.
'There it is!'

There was never any doubt in either of our minds.
The small grey cottage a mile away, squat in the lonely
landscape, surrounded by trees and edged into the side
of a hill, became as if by magic the present and the
future. It was as if a magician beside this ancient Carn
had cast a spell upon us, so that we could touch the
future as we could, at that moment, touch the Carn.
There in the distance we could see our figures moving
about our daily tasks, a thousand, thousand figures
criss-crossing the untamed land, dissolving into each
other, leaving a mist of excitement of our times to come.

The American *Look* magazine called Jeannie 'the prettiest publicity girl in the world'; and when it was announced she was leaving the Savoy, the newspapers wrote about her as if they were saying goodbye to a star. A columnist in the *Daily Mail* described her as slim, colleen-like, with green eyes and dark hair:

– who seems so young, innocent and delicately pretty that you couldn't imagine her saying 'Boo' to the smallest and silliest goose. But Jean has said 'Boo' to all sorts of important people including tough American correspondents.

For ten years she has been a key woman at that international rendezvous of film stars, politicians, maharajahs, financiers, business men and what have you – the Savoy Hotel.

It was nearly midnight, on our first weekend, when we reached Penzance. A gale was blowing in from the sea and as we drove along the front cascades of spray drenched the car as if coming from a giant hose. We crossed Newlyn Bridge, then up steep Paul Hill and along the winding road past the turn of Lamorna Valley; then up another hill, Boleigh Hill, where King Athelstan fought the Cornish ten centuries ago. Rain was whipping the windscreen when we turned off the road along a lane, through the dark shadows of a farm, until it petered out close to the cliff's edge. I got out and opened a gate, then drove bumpily across a field with the headlights swathing a way through a carpet of escaping rabbits. This, the back entrance to Minack, was the way we had to use until the bramble covered lane was opened up again; and after I pulled up beside a stone hedge, we still had two fields to scramble across in the darkness and the rain and the gale before we reached the cottage that was now to be our home.

I lit a candle and the light quivered on the peeling, yellow-papered walls. Everything was the same as the day we first pushed open the door; the ancient Cornish range, the pint-sized rooms with their matchbox thick divisions, the wooden floor peppered with holes – only it was raining now and above the howl of the gale was the steady drip, drip of water from the leaking roof.

We didn't care. The adventure had begun.

The full moon was waiting to greet us at Minack, a soft breeze came from the sea and the Lizard light winked every few seconds across Mount's Bay. An owl hooted in the wood and afar off I heard the wheezing bark, like a hyena, of a vixen. A fishing boat chugged by, a mile offshore, its starboard light bright on the mast. It was very still. The boulders, so massive in the day, had become gossamer in the moonlight, and the cottage, so squat and solid, seemed to be floating in the centuries of its past.

I said to Jeannie: 'Let's see if Monty will come for a walk.'

He came very slowly down the lane, peering suddenly at dangers in the shadows, sitting down and watching us, then softly stepping forward. His white shirt-front gleamed like a lamp. He sniffed the air, his little nose puzzling the source of the scents of water weeds, blue-bells and the sea. He found a log and clawed it, arching his back. He heard the rustle of a mouse and he became

tense, alert to pounce. I felt as I watched him that he was an adventurer prying his private unknown, relishing the prospect of surprise and of the dangers which would be of his own making.

We paused by the little stream, waiting for him to join us and, when he did, he rubbed his head affectionately against my leg, until suddenly he saw the pebbles of the moonlight on the water. He put out a paw as if to touch them.

'I'll pick him up and carry him over.'

But when I bent down to do so he struggled free of my grasp – and with the spring of a panther he leapt across, and dashed into the shadows beyond.

'Well done!' we cried, 'well done!'

This little stream where it crosses the lane as if it were the moat of Minack, halting the arrival of strangers, greeting us on our returns, acting as the watch of our adventures, was given a name that night.

Monty's Leap.

April passed, the potato season drew near and the inhabitants of the district, including ourselves, began to develop the mood of prospectors in a gold rush.

Three or four times a day Jeannie and I inspected the land which Tommy Williams had planted with one and a half tons of seed – the small meadows he had cut out of the top of the cliff, and the upper part of the cemetery field. The sight fascinated us. We stood and stared at the dark green leaves, hypnotised by their coarse texture, greedily calculating the amount of the harvest; then we would bend down and tickle a plant, stirring the earth round it with our hands, and calling out when we found a tiny potato.

'Need a nice shower,' Tommy would say, 'and they'll treble in size within a week.' Or in the lane, I would meet John who, in answer to the inevitable question: 'How are the taties looking?' would say gloomily, 'Been known for a gale to come at this stage . . . blast them black and only the weight of seed been lifted.' It was not only the size of the harvest which was at stake, but also its timing. There was a rivalry among growers as to who would be the first to draw, like jockeys at the starting gate; and the information that was circulated was as inspired as that on a racecourse. I would go up to Jim Grenfell's pub at St. Buryan in the evening and listen to the gossip.

'Bill Strick was cut by frost last night.'

'Over at Mousehole they look handsome.'

'Nothing will be going away until after Buryan Feast.'

'William Henry starts drawing Monday.'

These rumours and false alarms increased as the pace of excitement grew faster every day, and by the end of the month the inevitable question had become: 'Started drawing yet?'

The bright light of day had gone from the cliff when we reached it and the sun was dipping to the sea on the other side of the Penwith peninsula. The shadows of the rocks were enjoying their brief passage of life before dark, and the sea was dotted with the waking lights of the pilchard fleet. I poised the long-handled shovel and cumbersomely jabbed it under a plant, lifting the bundle of earth and tossing it to where Jeannie was standing. She stooped, shook the sturdy leaves, and ran her hand through the soil. And there, gleaming bright in the dusk, were six potatoes, each the comfortable size of a baby's fist.

Jeannie and I were up at dawn the following morning and I drove the Land-rover over the shoulder of the cemetery field and down to the top of the cliff. It was a heavenly morning with a haze hiding the horizon, the first swallows skimming the landscape, the white parasols of the may trees pluming from the green bracken, and the scent of bluebells mingling with the salt air of the sea. In the back of the car we had a spring balance weighing machine and a tripod on which to hang it, a bundle of chips and a ball of binder twine with which to tie the cardboard tops when the chips were full; a pair of scissors, the shovel, a box full of salesman's labels with printed addresses of different markets. It was a lush moment of hope, blissfully blinded from the realities the years would see.

The blessing of enthusiasm is its ability to deceive pleasantly.

During the days that followed, smoothly dressed salesmen appeared on the cliff, watching me dig and ache my way through a meadow, bantering me with news of prices better than their rivals.

'We paid 8½d. home at Bristol,' one would say, and then another two hours later would announce: 'Manchester is strong. We expect 9d. tomorrow.' They served too as the errand boys of news from other potato areas and I would clutter my worries over the prices with the threats that these areas, so much larger than our own, would soon be in production. These threats became progressively worse in their nature, beginning gently with: 'Marazion starts next week', edging dangerously to 'Gulval are opening up their fields' or the generalised black news that 'the farmers begin Tuesday', and growing to a climax with 'Jersey are at their peak' or 'Pembroke has a bumper crop.' And then, most disastrous of all, 'Lincoln has begun.' If you have not cleared the cliff by the time Lincoln stream their potato lorries to the markets, you might as well tip your potatoes in the sea. Nowadays these threats have become internationalised and one goes dizzy with the news that Covent

Garden is flooded with Morocco, Birmingham with Cyprus, Liverpool with Malta; and it is only when you hear that France has Colorado beetle and has stopped sending that you have a glimmer of hope.

The winds curl Minack in winter. In the beginning while we sat snug in the cottage a sense of security acted as a narcotic against the roar outside. A book, a pipe, the scent of a wood fire, Monty on my lap. There was comfort in joining the ghosts who had listened to the same rage, in sheltering within the walls that withstood centuries of siege. Then, as we passed through the shoals of first enthusiasms, facing the reality of the tasks we had undertaken, tension replaced comfort as the winds blew.

I am afraid now when the westerly comes galloping over the hill behind the cottage and charges with thundering hoofs into the elms that edge the wood; when the northerly steps aloofly along the valley, chilling its visit with frost; when the easterly bites from the Lizard, mouthing the sea and ripping our cliff which puts up a hand to stop it; when the southerly brings the rain and the storm which binds the sea and the land in gloom. For all are our enemies. Those from the east and the south carry salt as they blow, salt which films over flower petals and leaves and burns them papery white. The wind from the west savages the crops like a madman, and that from the north shivers black the plants in its way.

Jeannie spent the first winter locked in the chicken house we used as a spare bedroom, writing *Meet Me At The Savoy*. There was the camp bed used by her father in the 1914 war and now strewn with her papers, a rug, a secondhand kitchen table with her typewriter, an upturned box as a chair, and another box where a paraffin lamp hissed at night, except when the winds blew and then it was silent against the roar outside. 'Where's Jeannie?' friends who called would ask. 'In the chicken house,' I would answer, 'here's the key. Go and see if she wants to be let out.'

Up to the second week of March the weather had been soft and warm, so gentle the wind one could not believe the gales of winter had ever existed, or could ever come again. Our only concern was to pick the daffodils, bunch and send away. We had no time to anticipate trouble. We listened to the weather forecast but day after day it was so monotonously the same that there came an evening when we did not bother to turn on the wireless. The sky was clear, the sea still, and there was a pleasant security in the quietness, lulling us early to bed and quickly to sleep.

Suddenly I was awakened by a crash, and in the dimness I saw the curtains billowing before the open window like sails torn from the mast. I fumbled for my torch and at the same time Jeannie cried out: 'My face cream! That was my new bottle of Dorothy Gray I left by the window!'

I had time neither to sympathise, laugh nor investigate the damage. It was the Lizard wind hissing through the trees, tearing into the daffodils that were scheduled to be picked in the morning.

'Hurry,' I said. 'We must get down to the field . . .' and we pulled on our clothes and in a few minutes were fighting, heads down, against a gale that was to roar across Mount's Bay without pause for thirty-six hours. Our task was absurd, but ignorance at first made it appear feasible, the comfortable optimism at the beginning of a battle, the sheer stupidity of believing we could conquer the elements.

We had one torch which Jeannie held as I grappled at the waving stems, and unable to stand in the screaming wind we crawled on our hands and knees up and down the paths between the beds. For ten minutes we fought with the Hospodar and then, only a handful picked, I yelled to Jeannie: 'It's hopeless here . . . let's try the Coverack Glory!' Down we staggered to the lower part of the field and the beam of the torch shone on a sight which resembled a herd of terrified miniature animals tethered to the ground. Spray was now sticking to our faces and our hands, and a sense of doom was enveloping our hearts. We could not win. Nothing we could do would save our harvest.

Fishermen call the Lizard wind the starving wind, for the fish hide from it on the bed of the sea and the boats return empty to port. Landsmen solemnly call it the gizzard wind, as it bites into the body and leaves you tired when the day is still young. It is a hateful wind, no good to anybody, drying the soil into powdery dust, blackening the grass like a film of oil, punching the daffodils with the blows of a bully. It is seldom a savage wind as it was on the night it destroyed the Hospodar and Coverack Glory; if it were, if it spat its venom then recoiled into quiet, you could cry over the damage and forget. Instead, it simmers its fury like a man with a grudge, moaning its grievance on and on, day after day, remorselessly wearying its victim into defeat.

The wasted stems of the Hospodar and the Coverack Glory were piled high on the compost heap and now the Bernardino and Croesus hastened to join them. Nothing dramatic in their destruction, no sudden obliteration to grieve over; the wind bit at each bud as it unfurled from the calyx, flapping the edge of a petal until it turned brown; or it maliciously made the stems dance to its tune so that they swayed together hither and thither, the buds rubbing and chafing, bruising each other to an invisible end.

I sometimes wonder whether the ghosts of the cottage cast a spell over us, enabling us to accept this abuse of twentieth-century comfort in the way we did. Inconvenience had pervaded the cottage for over five hundred years, so was it inevitable that we should act as if it were natural? The twentieth century decorates life like a Christmas cake, but it still cannot do anything about the basic ingredients. And there seemed to be a starkness in our companionship which enabled us to find a fulfilment without the aid of man-made devices, as if the canvas of each day was so vast that mirror-smooth techniques of living, coma entertainment like television, would only make it unmanageable. We are still without electricity and we remain thankful we have no telephone; yet it would be a pose to pretend that self-denial did not seek its compensations.

We were aware that there was something else at stake besides material victory: there was the continuing challenge to prove that we were not flirting with the tedium of manual labour, that our enthusiasm had not been checked by reverses or by the roughness of the life, that we possessed staying power which could earn respect. It was a simple ambition and some would call it a valueless one, but within it there was the prospect of peace of mind born of permanence. There is no permanence in the conventional ambitions that hasten you up the pyramid of power, each step killing one ambition and creating another, leading you by a noose to a pinnacle where, too late, you look back on the trampled path and find the yearning within you is the same when you were young.

'What on earth's wrong with Monty tonight?' And I bent down to pick him up. He darted to the door and when I moved to open it, rushed to the sofa, forking his claws in the side, raking the material, and earning a 'Shut up, Monty!' from Jeannie. There was a sound outside as if a car was driving up to the cottage. 'Listen,' I said, and we paused, tense. 'It's a plane,' said Jeannie, relieved. There it was again, a rushing, moaning sound. 'It isn't,' I answered knowledgeably, 'it's the wind.'

It was the sound of the scouts, the fingers of the

wind, stretching ahead, probing the hills and woods, the rocks and hedges, the old cottages, the lonely trees acting as sentinels of the land. They probe and jab, searching for flying leaves, decaying branches ready to fall, for flowers youthfully in bloom, for the green swath of the potato tops; and finding, they rush on searching for more, magnificently confident that the majesty of the gale which follows will crush and pound and obliterate. And when they have gone there is an instant of stillness to remind you of a quiet evening, the passing assurance of a safe world, and you wait. You wait and wonder if you were wrong and the wind is innocent; you listen, your mind peeling across the green meadows whose defences are impotent; then suddenly the slap of the face and the braying hounds of hell and the heaving mountain of maniacal power.

The gale roared without pause till the afternoon of 29 March, vicious, friendless and with frost in its scream. Here was man as helpless as the foam on the rocks, centuries of rising conceit contemptuously humbled, the joke of the tempest. Action was masochistic. We struggled heads down as if fighting a way through invisible jungle grass, buffeted, pushed back, soundless in our shouting, kneeling to the ground to gape at a meadow in its progress towards obliteration; then we hustled home as if our coats were kites, running without effort, feathers in air.

We sat and waited. The vapid wait, droning the hours away with our fears, calculating losses, listening to the ships' waveband as vessels neared Land's End – 'I don't fancy going round the corner.' Unknown voices sharing our company, leaping to the window when the noise

for a second abated, hearing the sea hissing like a coast-
line of cobras, sleeping with demons in our dreams.
Waiting, waiting, waiting. And when it was over, when
our ears were still humming with the beating drums of
fury and the sea still heaved in mud-grey valleys, we
went out into an afternoon that had suddenly become
as caressing as a summer's day; as if a lost temper had
been replaced by shame and the cost of havoc was being
guiltily assessed. The Minack potato meadows were a
pattern of black stumps, pocketsize havens the wind had
entered like a tornado, and there were gaps where not
even stumps were to be seen. At Pentewan, the army of
green, plants the size of cabbages had become a foot-
high petrified forest, drooping in the sunshine like melting black candles. Black also was the grass on the banks,
filmed as if with tar, and the stinging nettles which once
taunted us to scythe them down; and here and there
wild daffodils stared forlornly, with petals shredded into
tea-stained strips; or with necks broken, their heads
drooped against the stems like victims of the gallows.
The desolation looked up at the blue sky and the fleck
of a lark singing. A magpie flew by chattering coarsely,
and for a second I saw a fox silhouetted on a rock above
the quarry. A boat chugged by outward bound to the
fishing grounds beyond the Isles of Scilly, and we
looked down at the men on deck as if we were on a hill
and they in a valley. Normality was returning even if
the thrash of the whip was still in our ears. Ideas began
to form, and the warm challenge born of disaster quick-
ened our minds.

Jeannie did not reply and we began to walk arm in arm up the fields towards the cottage. The silence hurt both of us. We had been consumed by the mission I had just fulfilled, and now we were left with thoughts that frightened us. We had not only lost our gamble, but were faced with retrieving its cost without anyone to help us. We had not bargained for failure when we left London, and its arrival, the sudden barefacedness of its arrival, brought unbearable depression.

And then, just as we gloomily reached the old stone stable and the slope which led up to the cottage, Jeannie suddenly said in a voice that sounded as if our problems had been solved: 'Look! There's a gull on the roof!'

He was to us the symbol we needed. The sight of him reassured us in the sense that at this moment of material defeat, the wild had suddenly accepted us as it had accepted the generations who had toiled at Minack before us. The gull had watched and now was prepared to trust. We had never attempted to lure him. We had never noticed him before. He was one of hundreds who flew every day in the sky above Minack, and he had chosen this moment of distress to adopt us. It was from that time that we felt we belonged to Minack, that we were no longer interlopers from the city imposing ourselves on the countryside, pretending in fact to be country people. We had passed the test. We were no longer looking on from the outside, armchair escapists who believe that dreams are real. We had been defeated, and there would be no soft way out for victory. We had joined the ghosts of Minack in the endless struggle against the seasons and, in doing so, we had embraced all the things they had seen and heard and done. We had become part of the ageless continuity of Minack; and the gull on the roof was its symbol.

A Cat in the Window

'This is diabolical,' I said in pretence fury, addressing *Jeannie and Lois, 'and don't think I haven't a card up my sleeve ... I'm going to chuck this thing over Hammersmith Bridge on the way home.'* I spoke so *vehemently that Lois seemed half to believe me. 'Yes I am,'* I said, rubbing it in. *'I'll stop the car and fling the cat over the parapet.'*

I first met Monty in Room 205 of the Savoy Hotel. He was six weeks old, and when I came into the room was tumbling, chasing, biting an old typewriter ribbon dragged temptingly across the carpet by Lois, Jeannie's secretary. He was the size and colour of a handful of crushed autumn bracken. At the time I did not notice the distinguishing marks I was later to know so well – the silky-white shirt front, the smudge of orange on the left paw, the soft maize colour of the fur on his tummy. I did not notice his whiskers, nor his tail with its dark rings against cream, the rings graduating in size to the tip which, in his lifetime, was to flick this way and that, a thousand, thousand times. I saw only a pretty kitten with great big innocent eyes gambolling in the incongruous setting of Jeannie's office, and I wondered why.

'What's this?' I said to Lois, looking down at the two of them. 'What on earth is this kitten doing here?' I had seen ambassadors, film stars, famous journalists, politicians of all parties in Jeannie's office, but I had never before met a cat. It made me suspicious.

'Come on,' I said, 'come on, Lois, tell me what it's all about?' But Lois, the perfect secretary, went on playing as if she hadn't heard me. 'Lois, you're hiding something from me. Where's Jeannie? What's she been up to? Both of you know I dislike cats and if . . .'

'She'll be back soon.' Lois was smiling and refusing to be drawn. 'She had to go over to Claridge's. General Montgomery has just arrived and nobody is allowed to know. She won't be long.' As public relations officer of the Savoy Group, it was part of Jeannie's job to keep certain news from the Press, just as much as it was on other occasions to get items of news widely publicised.

But on this occasion, on this particular warm, summer afternoon, as I awaited her return with Lois and the chocolate box cover of a kitten, her task was specially important.

Monty had arrived to make a progress report to Churchill on the Battle of the Desert.

I was determined to hold fast to my traditional dislike of the species. I was not going to be hypnotised by gentle purrs, soft kneading of paws, an elegant walk across the room and a demand to jump on my knees. I disliked cats. I most certainly would not have one in our home after we had married.

This was my mood as I waited for Jeannie to return from Claridge's. We had been married three months.

But I made no scene except a mock one. It was an inevitable defeat. I could only bluster. I could not enter my married life with an argument about a cat.

Monty chose the moment of Jeannie's return to pounce upon the toe of my shoe, then disappear up my trousers, except for a tail. He tickled my leg until I had to stoop and, for the first time, touch him. Jeannie and Lois watched hopefully the effect this would have on me. He was very soft, and the wriggle with which he tried to escape me was feeble, like the strength of my little finger. I felt the teeth nibble my hand, and a tiny claw trace a tickle on my skin; and when I picked him up and held him firmly in front of me, the big eyes stared childishly at me with impotent resentment. I had never held a cat in my hands before.

'This is diabolical,' I said in pretence fury, addressing Jeannie and Lois, 'and don't think I haven't a card up my sleeve . . . I'm going to chuck this thing over Hammersmith Bridge on the way home.' I spoke so vehemently that Lois seemed half to believe me. 'Yes I am,' I said, rubbing it in. 'I'll stop the car and fling the cat over the parapet.'

'Kitten,' murmured Lois.

'Monty,' said Jeannie.

There is no defence against women who sense your heart has already surrendered. The head, however astute in presenting its arguments, appears hollow. If Jeannie wanted Monty she had to have him. How could I deny her? The best I could do was to learn to tolerate his existence; and make an attempt to impose conditions.

'All right, I won't do that,' I said, and was immediately irked by the gleam of victory in their eyes. 'But I'll tell you what I will do . . .' I looked defiantly at both of them. 'I'll make quite certain he is a kitchen cat. There'll be no question of him wandering about the house as if he owns it.'

On reflection, I believe my dislike was based on their independence. A dog, any dog, will come to you wagging its tail with friendliness if you click your fingers or call to it. There is no armed neutrality between the dog world and the human race. If a human is in need of affection and there is a dog about, he is sure to receive it, however frail affection from a stranger may be. Dogs are prepared to love; cats, I believed, were not.

I had observed, too, that cat owners (but who, I wondered, would call himself the owner of a cat?) were apt to fall into two types. Either they ignored the cat, put it out at night whatever the weather, left it to fend for itself when they went away on holidays and treated it, in fact, as a kind of better class vermin; or else they worshipped the animal like a god. The first category appeared callous; the second devoid of sense.

I had seen, for instance, a person sit rigid and uncomfortable in a chair because a cat had chosen his lap as the whim of its own particular comfort. I had noticed, and been vexed by the hostess who hastens away at the end of a meal with titbits for the cat which has stared balefully at her guests during the course of it. Cats, it seemed to me, hinted aloofly the power of hypnotism; and as if in an attempt to ward off this uncanniness, their owners pandered to them, anxiously trying to win approval for themselves by flattery, obedience, and a curious vocabulary of nonsensical phrases and noises. A cat lover, I had found, was at the mercy of the cat.

As soon as I picked him out of the wicker basket in which we had brought him home to Thames Bank Cottage on the river at Mortlake, I explained to our housekeeper that Monty was to be a kitchen cat. 'I don't want to see him at all,' I said. 'He's here to catch mice and, although he may be small for that yet, I've been told the very smell of a cat will keep them away.'

I looked at Jeannie. She was busily unwrapping a small paper parcel. 'Isn't that true? Didn't you say that?'

'Oh yes . . . yes.'

An object had now appeared from the paper. A small sole *bonne femme*. It was freshly cooked and succulent.

'Good heavens, Jeannie,' I said, 'where did you get that?'

'Latry gave it to me,' she said. Latry was the famous *maître chef* of the Savoy. 'He's cooked it specially as a celebration present for Monty.' I looked at the fish and then at Monty. Only a few hours before, the girl in the hairdressers was frightened he would be put away on the morrow.

'Really, Jeannie,' I said crossly, 'you can't go cadging food for the cat.'

'I wasn't cadging. Latry gave it to me, I tell you. He loves cats and felt honoured to cook Monty's first meal.'

'Honoured,' I murmured to myself, and shuddered.

Monty played his own part very well because from the beginning he made it plain he liked me. It was a dangerous moment of flattery when I realised this and, I believe, had it not been for my entrenched posture of dislike for the species, I would have fallen for it without more ado. There was, however, a thick enough layer of prejudice inside me for me to hold out.

He twisted his head as if he were going to fold up in a ball, collapsed on the floor and turned over, and lay with his back on the green carpet, paws in the air, displaying his silky maize underparts while a pair of bright yellow eyes hopefully awaited the pleasure the sight would give me. The reward he expected was a gentle stroke until he decided he had had one too many when there would be a savage mock attempt to bite my fingers.

But on this first occasion I was holding a pipe cleaner in my hand and I tickled him with that, which led to a game, which led half an hour later to his sitting on my desk, a large kidney-shaped Regency desk with a top like a table, performing ridiculous antics with a pencil.

I was sitting there roaring with laughter when the door opened. In walked Jeannie.

My capitulation was complete, and within a few

weeks there was no pretence that Monty was a kitchen
cat.

On the night a near miss blew the roof off, leaving our
sitting-room facing the stars; we were not in the shelter.
It was the evening of our first wedding anniversary and a
number of friends were celebrating with us when we
heard the stick coming ... one, two, three, four and
wham! The Mortlake Brewery had a direct hit and the
fire that followed lit the night into daylight, and we
knew that this tempting sight might lead to another
attack. None of us was hurt, only covered with plaster,
but the room we loved so much was a terrible sight.
Jeannie and I were standing at the door looking at it,
thinking how only an hour or two before we had spent
such care getting it ready, when suddenly she said:
'Where's Monty?'

We ran down the stairs asking as we went whether
anyone had seen him. We ran into the kitchen shouting
his name, then into the dining-room, then into the spare
bedroom, that led from the kitchen. No one had seen
him. I ran into the garden calling his name, the guns still

firing, the flames in the Brewery leaping into the sky; and I remembered how even in that moment of distress I found myself marvelling at the silhouette of a fireman's ladder that was already poised high against the fire, a pin-point of a man at the top of it. 'Monty,' I yelled, 'Monty!' No sign of him there so I went back to the house asking everyone to look, then out on to the river bank where I knew Jeannie had gone. I found her, but no Monty; and after searching for a while we felt our task hopeless, nothing to do except go home and wait. 'He'll turn up,' I said, trying to encourage her.

And half an hour later, into the kitchen came one of our guests, a burly Australian war correspondent, with Monty held in his arms like a child. His fur was powdered with plaster, as white as if he had spent the night in a bakery house.

'He'd got in his foxhole,' the Australian said, with a grin on his face, using the phrase of a soldier. 'I found him upstairs in the airing cupboard!'

It was at the time of Monty's return from Jeannie's mother in St Albans, that he developed a growl. Most cats growl at some time or other but it is a sound that is a close cousin to a purr. Monty's growl was a deep-throated challenge of such resonance that he might have acquired it from one of the larger dogs he hated. Yet it was not a weapon of war, a threat to frighten an opponent.

It was a means of self reassurance, a method of bolstering himself when he found himself in a situation not to his liking. Any odd noise he did not understand would bring forth the growl and, for that matter, any big noise too. He growled at the guns which fired at the flying bombs, and at thunder, and when rockets took the place of flying bombs he growled at them. The first rocket which ever landed in Britain landed within a mile of Mortlake; and it is Monty's growl I remember, not the explosion.

In the years which followed the end of the war we were seldom at home in the evenings except at weekends. The nature of our work rushed us from party to party and we used to return home increasingly exhausted as the week developed.

Monty would glare at us from inside the dining-room window as we arrived home, the sweep of the headlights shining on his fierce face. 'We're in trouble again,' I would say as I put the key in the door. It was perfectly true that he had the knack of making us feel we had misbehaved, that two o'clock in the morning was a disgraceful hour to return home. We would switch on the lights and hurry into the dining-room ready to gush a greeting, only to find he had not moved, that he was still staring out of the window pretending to be unaware of our arrival, except for the sharp flicks of his tail.

Monty's big day in the dining-room window was Boat Race day.

Both Jeannie and I were Cambridge supporters, and before our first Boat Race party Jeannie had bought Monty a large light-blue ribbon which she tied in a bow round his neck. I did not approve. I thought such a gesture was ostentatious and silly and I anticipated confidently that Monty would wriggle free from the encumbrance as soon as he had the chance. He did not do so. True the ribbon became more and more askew as the day wore on, with the bow finishing up under his tummy, but this had nothing to do with any action on his part. It was the attention he received which caused that.

Hence the light-blue ribbon became an annual ritual and invariably, after the bow had been tied, he would sit in the dining-room window staring with a lordly air at the crowds; and the crowds looking for a diversion until the race began would call to him and shout to their friends about him. He adored this period of glory: so much on his own but now at last receiving his due. And when our guests arrived, a hundred or more packing the cottage, a cacophony of laughter and talk, cigarette smoke clouding the rooms, people sitting on the floor and the stairs, glasses everywhere, Jeannie and I rushing around with bottles and plates of cold food, Monty was as cool as a cucumber. He would stroll from room to room, pausing beside a guest when the praise was high, even deigning to jump on a lap, ignoring the cat haters, refusing with well-bred disgust any morsel dangled before him by some well-meaning admirer. He was unobtrusively sure of himself; and when the rackety day was over, when Jeannie and I had gone to bed feeling too tired to sleep and we put out a hand and touched him at the bottom of the bed, we both felt safe. Safe, I mean, from the tensions among which we lived.

There was an occasion when he travelled as a stowaway

on the night train to Penzance from Paddington. Jeannie was always very proud of this exploit as she was the architect of its success. She was due to join me for the weekend and was dining at the Savoy before catching her sleeper, when suddenly she decided she would like Monty to accompany her. She dashed back to Mortlake, found him, after a five-minute desperate search, crouched on the wall at the end of the garden, and arrived at Paddington with three minutes to spare. Monty was an admirable conspirator. He remained perfectly still as she rushed him along the platform wrapped in a rug. Not a miaow. Not a growl. And nobody would ever have known that the night train had carried a cat, had Jeannie been able to curb her vociferous enthusiasm when she arrived at Penzance.

But she behaved as if the Crown Jewels were in her compartment. She was in such a high state of excitement when I met her, that she did not notice the car attendant was directly behind me as she slid open the door to disclose her secret.

Monty's aplomb was superb. He stared at the man with regal indifference from the bunk. And as I recovered from my surprise and Jeannie muttered feeble excuses, all the car attendant found himself able to say was: 'Good heavens, what a beautiful cat!'

Five minutes later we were in the car on the road to Minack.

Monty's transition into a country cat was a gradual affair. An urban gentleman does not become a country gentleman simply by changing his clothes. He must learn to adopt a new code of manners and a new approach to the outdoors; to be less suave and to show more bluster, to accept the countryside as a jungle which has to be mastered by skill and experience. Monty, as an urban cat, had therefore a lot to learn.

There were the unsolicited purrs. A cat has to be in a very bad mood if a human cannot coax him to purr. There is little honour in this achievement, only the satisfaction that a minute or two is being soothed by such a pleasant sound. But the unsolicited purrs belong to quite another category. These are the jewels of the cat fraternity, distributed sparingly like high honours in a kingdom. They are brought about by great general contentment. No special incident induces them. No memory of past or prospect of future banquets. Just a whole series of happy thoughts suddenly combine together and whoever is near is lucky enough to hear the result. Thus did Monty from time to time reward us.

As Monty grew older his contentment was so obvious for all to see that we felt part of it. If something had gone wrong, if we had suffered some defeat which left us despondent, the sight of his magnificent person poised perhaps on some wall with the sun glinting his red bracken coat, his head alertly surveying the scene around him, would be enough to quell our momentary fears. His example was a positive contribution to the life we had chosen for ourselves.

In spring, Monty's thick coat began to moult and we used to give him a daily combing. He would lie on my lap as I traced the comb up and down his back, on his sides and up and around the jowls of his neck. He loved it. He purred happily until I turned him over and began the same task on his underparts. There would now be silence except for a series of little grunts. He found it awkward to purr on his back.

And when it was all over I would collect the silky fur in my hand, go outside and throw it into the wind. It floated into the air, soaring and billowing, eddying in the end to some thorn bush or tussock of grass or entangling itself in the sea pinks on the wall. It did not stay in any of these places for long. The fur was much sought after. Most nests around Minack were lined with it.

Time deceives in its pace, luring years into yesterdays, garlanding memories without intervals, seeping the knowledge of age into one's mind. I did not want to say how old Monty was. I did not want to remember that for so long he had been the recipient of our secret thoughts. Each of us had talked to him in that mood of abandon which is safe within friendship. Maybe it was only a cat's friendship, but secure and never to be tarnished, easing problems because the aftermath of confession did not breed the fears of disclosure.

He was an integral part of our successes and failures at Minack, and a hulky miner from St Just whom we once had helping us called him the foreman. 'Look out, the foreman's coming,' he would shout as he lunged away with his shovel in a potato meadow. 'We'll get our cards if we don't do our job properly.' Monty would appear and walk leisurely down the row where he had been digging, sniffing the discarded potato tops spreadeagled on the side, as if he were checking that all the potatoes had been collected from the plants. It was always a solemn inspection. There were no games. And when he had completed it, and had left the meadow, disappearing out of sight, the hulky miner would stab his shovel into the ground, rub his hands together and call out: 'All clear, boys. We can have a smoke now.'

It was in daffodil time that his illness began to threaten the normality of his days. Nothing sudden, no pain, just a gradual ebbing of strength; so that first the bluebell walk to the Carn had to be abandoned, then the one we used to take along the top of the cliff, and then even the strolls to the Leap became less frequent. I would watch him from the corner of the cottage wending his way down the lane, and my heart would yearn to see a spring in his movements I knew I would never see again. He would reach the stream, drink a little, then turn and come slowly back. This stroll was the yardstick of our hopes, and sometimes Jeannie would come running to me: 'He's been twice to the Leap this morning!' . . . and her voice would have the tone that the inevitable was going to be defeated.

He died on a lovely May morning in his sixteenth year. I had hurried to fetch the vet and on my return I found Jeannie had taken him out into the warm sun and he was breathing gently on a bed of lush green grass. Up above on the roof was Hubert, the gull, quite still, his feathers bunched, as if he were waiting for something; and within a yard or two of Monty were his friends; Charlie, the chaffinch, and Tim, the robin. No sound from either of them. Tim on a rosebush, Charlie on a grey rock. They were strange mourners for a cat.

The next day, soon after the sun had risen above the Lizard far away across Mount's Bay, we carried him down the lane to the stream and buried him beside it. Between his paws we placed a card:

Here lies our beloved friend Monty who, beside the stream that crosses the lane and is known as Monty's Leap, is forever the guardian of Minack.

A Drake at the Door

Thus Jeannie and I would be there with these three who had the promise of the years before them, each helping us, each so full of secret thoughts and hopes, puzzled, contradictory, timid and brave, obstinate and imaginative. I understood why Jeannie said to me one day that she was grateful for the necessity of cutting lettuces; a humble task, perhaps, but there was more to gain than the price received.

Jane was with us now. She had knocked at the door of the cottage one August evening the year before while Jeannie and I were having supper. She wore jeans, sandals, and a dark-blue fisherman's jersey. Hair, like a pageboy's, the colour of corn, fell to her shoulders. She was tiny, and yet there was about her a certain air of assurance, a hint of worldly confidence which belied her child-like appearance. She was fourteen years old.

'I'm Jane Wyllie,' she announced, 'I want to work for you.'

There was no sound of the soil in her voice. It was a bell, a softly pitched bell; and her words came pealing out in a rush, as if they had been rehearsed, as if a pause would break the spell of childish enthusiasm with which she was flooding the cottage. Neither Jeannie nor I dared interrupt. We had to wait until her role had been played, watching blue eyes that seemed to lurk with laughter, paying proper attention to an intense performance designed to prove her services would be invaluable.

Her plot was a simple one; for Jeannie and I were to be the means by which she would be able to leave school. We were the pivot of her future. If she could win us, total strangers as we were, over to her side she would be able to defeat any array of schoolmistresses, relations and friends who were urging her to pursue a scholastic career. We were, therefore, unsuspectingly the ace up her sleeve. We sat in innocence and listened.

She was at a boarding school near Salisbury and as she would be fifteen that November she would be old enough to leave at the end of the winter term. Her headmistress looked upon the prospect with displeasure, because it seemed she possessed the kind of brains which could be moulded into the pursuit of a conventional career. At this point, unknowingly of course, she had struck a chord of sympathy in both Jeannie and myself.

Both of us carried the memory of youthful rebellion, and neither of us had ever regretted it. Jane had begun to seep into our affections.

I looked at her as she sat neatly on the edge of a chair. She was dainty, small hands and feet, and although her figure was sturdy she did not suggest the stamina for a landgirl.

'What does your mother say?'

'Mum's not quite certain, but if I get a job . . .'

Her mother was in the quandary of all mothers. The age of breaking away, the taut arguments which swing this way and that, the rampaging emotions of love and responsibility, so anxious to act for the best, not to be selfish, not to yield to the temptation of keeping a child at home when the horizons await.

'Mum wants me to do what I feel I want to do, and I want to work on a flower farm.'

No wonder we were the ace up her sleeve. Five minutes' walk over the fields and she would be home. A job, in fact, on her doorstep. A home where her mother would be with her and her animals around her. We were her only chance. There was no other market garden in the neighbourhood who would need her; and neither did we.

'Jane,' I said gently, 'you see we don't need anyone like you. I've a man helping me and I don't want anyone else.'

She flushed, and her eyes wandered away from mine.

Geoffrey was our mainstay at the time. His home was in our village of St Buryan where generations of his family had lived. He was in his early thirties, strong as an ox, and the fastest picker of daffodils I have ever seen. He raced through a bed of daffodils as if he were some special machine devised to do the work automatically. The art of such picking lies in turning your hand backwards, burying it in the foliage, then moving forward, braking the stems off at the base until your hand can hold no more; each handful is dropped on the path and collected into the basket when the length of the bed has been completed. As always, the final skill lies in instinct. Geoffrey had an uncanny knack of inevitably picking the right stem; for myself, if I tried to go too fast, I would curse myself for picking a daffodil still green in bud.

He was a good shovel man. This is an outworn phrase today but, when we launched our ambitions at Minack, a man who was so described by his fellow villagers was among the labouring élite. The area was greatly dependent on cliff meadows and such meadows could not be dealt with by machine. The long Cornish shovel was the master. It turned the ground in the autumn, it planted potatoes, it dug them out, and in August it was at work again planting the daffodil bulbs.

'He's a good shovel man,' therefore became a testimony as powerful as one given to a Rolls-Royce engine.

And then there was Shelagh.

We first met her in the square outside St Buryan Church and we left her on that occasion without knowing her name or having any idea that she was to become for ever a part of Minack. We had A. P. Herbert staying with us at the time, and one morning when we had gone up the village a cluster of people had gathered around us, autograph books in hand, pressing A. P. H. for his signature.

'I'll give you a shilling if you can tell me who I am,' smiled A. P. H., taking her notebook and beginning to scribble. Shelagh blushed confusedly and looked down at the ground.

'Sir Hubert . . . or something,' she blurted out.

Even then, unknowingly, she had become a part of Minack. For a gull that summer had begun to haunt our cottage, sweeping inland every day from the cliffs, perching on the roof, watching us as we went about our business, splendidly emphasising a sense of community with the wild.

It was up there on the roof that morning we returned from St Buryan. We drove up the lane in the Land-rover, pulled up outside the cottage and, as I switched off the engine, the gull suddenly put back its head pointing its beak to the sky, and began to bellow the noise of a bird-like hyena.

'That,' said A. P. H. in mock solemnity, 'is a protest against my being called Sir Hubert . . . or something.'

From then on the gull had its name. For no other reason than this he was known to the end of his days as Hubert. He had a long time to go; and, as I will tell, Shelagh was with us when one day years later he came to us dying, shot through the foot by an airgun.

Shelagh left school the following year and went to work as a domestic help on a farm. We seldom saw her. A year or so later she left to join a number of girls on a large flower farm near Penzance; and, in order to save her money on the bus fare, she used to bicycle to and from St Buryan, up and down the hills, undeterred however bad the weather.

One day, as she was leaving work, her bicycle skidded and she fell off, so injuring her head that she was for ten days on the danger list. It was, of course, some weeks before she was fit again to work and by this time she had lost her job. One morning she arrived whitefaced at our door. She looked as if a long period of convalescence was essential.

But I knew without her speaking why she had come. Jobs are difficult to find for girls in West Cornwall and so it was inevitable that she should think of us. She had walked the three miles from St Buryan; and if during this walk she had been reciting to herself the phrases she planned to use, all she now could blurt out was:

'Have you got a job for me?'

There was no job. She was just too late.

'You see,' I explained, before driving her back to St Buryan in the Land-rover, 'we have just taken on a young girl, Jane . . . Jane Wyllie.'

I wish I had known at that moment that these two were to become such close friends. The lost look on Shelagh's face would not have been necessary.

The first task we gave Jane was looking after the sweet peas in the long greenhouse in front of the cottage. We had sown the seeds in September and transplanted the sturdy little plants in October. Now in January they were speedily climbing their supporting strings, and requiring the same persistent attention as painters give to the Forth Bridge.

They were scheduled to flower early in April; and we had chosen this crop, after earnest discussion with our horticultural advisers, because the greenhouse was unheated and sweet peas were certain to withstand the limited cold that might be expected in our area. We had not, however, forseen the labour they would involve.

The shoots had endlessly to be pinched out, and when you have two thousand plants the extent of this mammoth task can become a nightmare. Not for Jane. She used to disappear into the greenhouse at eight o'clock in the morning and still be there at five in the evening, day after day. And when periodically I used to open the door and call for her, an answer would come from somewhere in the jungle of green like the squeak of a rabbit:

'Yes?'

'Are you all right?'

'Yes, thank you.'

I met her mother one day, after a month of this, and asked her how she thought Jane was enjoying herself. I felt sorry that her first task was proving so dull. It was very useful but dull.

'Oh,' said her mother, 'you don't have to worry. Do you know what she said to me yesterday? She said: "Mum, while I was among the sweet peas today I thought how lucky I was to be doing what I've wanted to do all my life." '

I find it a little awesome when one puts in motion a large plan from which there is no turning back, and I was in this mood when I watched the end of the elms. It made me sensitive to the sadness of losing the trees. They had welcomed us when we first came to Minack, and I was now their executioner. I could not treat them briskly as inanimate objects which happened to bar my progress. They were entities of our life. I could not watch their end without sentiment. They had received our fresh eyes of enthusiasm and now were the victims of inescapable reality.

The greenhouse, except for the foundation of cement and breeze blocks, had arrived altogether on a lorry that edged down the lane with its cargo peering high above the hedge, the glass in vast packing cases, the cedarwood structure in numerous bundles. It was a terrifying sight. The lorry crept down the hill stopping every few yards halted by boulders on the edge of the lane which caught the wide wheels. It would back, the driver would twist his steering wheel, and then forward again, bumping and slithering towards Minack. It turned the last corner, straightened up for the last two hundred yards, and then I knew the really dangerous moment had arrived. A stretch lay ahead like a miniature causeway with a ditch on either side. Was it wide enough? Had we made a mistake when we built this part of the lane?

For this lorry, in a fashion, was making a maiden voyage. Only a few weeks before, the lane had been changed from the appearance of the dried-up bed of a turbulent river, into a surface fit for a limousine. Up until then we had called it our chastity belt. It had been impassable for private cars and rough enough for the Land-rover to make us hesitate to go out on trivial errands. We had been contained in a world of our own choosing, voluntary prisoners whose object was to be screened from the kind of life we had left.

In the summer Jane once again disappeared into the greenhouse, tending the tomatoes.

We had seven hundred plants of a variety called Moneymaker in eight long rows. Each had a string attached, like the sweet peas, around which the stem had to be twisted as the plant grew; and each had to have their shoots continually pinched out so that the main stem was left to grow on its own. Then at a later stage the plants were defoliaged.

It was easy to teach Jane what to do. Jeannie or I had only to show her something once for her to grasp the idea, and probably improve on it. She watched plants, any plants she was looking after, as if they were individuals; and so if a tomato plant, for instance, showed signs of a fault, she was quick to notice it.

'Mr Tangye?'

'Yes, Jane?'

I would be standing at the greenhouse door and from somewhere in the green foliage in front of me piped her small voice.

'The thirty-first plant in the third row from the right shows signs of botrytis on its stem.'

Jane had an unreliable sense of time. Both she and her mother had a strange effect on watches. I believe this sometimes happens when people have a surfeit of electricity in their bodies; but whatever the reason no watch would keep correct time for these two. Hence Jane would occasionally arrive for work at unconventional hours. Sometimes very early, sometimes very late.

Of course, it did not matter her being late because she could make up the time at the end of the day. Indeed, she was never a clock-watcher. She always stayed on until the job was finished. But in the beginning, when she was late, when she did not know what our reaction might be, she used to creep along like a Red Indian, keeping out of sight behind hedges, reaching Minack by a roundabout route; and hoping that she could begin work without her absence having been noted. She did this out of adventure, not out of guile. She always told us in the end.

It is a sweet moment when a long-awaited harvest awakes. It shares the common denominator of pleasure which embraces all endeavours that have taken a long time to plan, to nurture, and which then suddenly bursts before your eyes in achievement. You are no longer an onlooker waiting impatiently. The harvest is there to give you your reward; the fact of it destroys your worries and galvanises you into action. I know of few things so evergreen sweet as the first picking of a new crop.

I wonder sometimes which of the Walter Mittys in me I was looking for. It is easy to become so immersed in

day-to-day events that you lose sight of yourself. It is a
chronic disease. A daze of living. The twentieth century
speeds faster and faster and the pace only allows you to
live in perpetual disguise.

I could not pretend I had any lilt in deciding which
tractor to buy. The acquisition would be a burden.
There would be no prospect of some light-hearted compensation. It was not a foolish venture of frivolous
intent. It was utilitarian. A lump of metal which would
remind me day after day of the penalties of expansion.
I was standing there, the wind sharp against my face,
being courted by an object I did not want; which would
prove irresistible. I was at a beginning that had no banners to welcome me. I had no feeling of faith, as I
watched, that what I was doing, what I was prepared
to gamble, what indeed were my secret hopes . . . that
any of these things were justified. I was being driven
by a force that did not belong to me, which I distrusted,
yet obeyed.

It is my weakness that I prefer to carry someone with
me instead of imposing my wishes. I find it easier to
appeal rather than to order. And if you have a concern
like ours, so small and intimate, it is more essential than
ever to have a spirit of co-operation. In my anxiety to
achieve this co-operation I find I usually expect too
much. I so desire to skirt the prospect of a mood on
the part of someone I am employing, that I fall into the
trap of failing to give clear orders, I prefer to rely on a

kind of telepathy. I state the position as I see it, then expect the individual concerned to react in the same way, wishfully and foolishly thinking that my tedious process of thought has been shared by the other. I forget that I was alone when I assessed the future; that I alone endure the strains of raising finance, of carrying the burden of a crop disaster, of hoping to see daylight in another year. I should not expect the wage-earner to feel and think as I do.

We used to hang on to the words of the old growers as attentively as we used to listen to prominent politicians at times of crisis. We would fuss over an old chap in a pub about the merits of wallflowers with the same zest as we once sat in the Savoy's Grill Bar hearing the confidential views of some editor:

'Mark my words,' the old chap would say, sipping his beer, 'wallflowers are a proper crop. Cheap seed, can treat 'em rough, quick to pick, and a shilling a bunch.'

This was the kind of remark we loved to hear. A high priest was talking. He was passing us on information as valuable as a bar of gold. We used to go back home to the cottage, take pencil and paper, and calculate; and the calculation used to make us dizzy with excitement. It was simple. If we grew several thousand wallflowers we really would not have to grow anything else.

I launched my grandiose plan before I had time for second thoughts. It was flamboyant. It had no relation to our financial resources but it projected an image of such likely security that the cost could look after itself.

I ordered two mobile greenhouses each seventy feet long and eighteen feet wide, and provisionally ordered two more.

This fling at the fates so intoxicated our imagination that we drew up a blueprint for the coming year, so vast in its scope that if it came off our material problems would be solved for ever. It was also sensible. We were not allowing our enthusiasm to interfere with our judgement. And yet, in retrospect I wonder if our gesture was not prompted by an emotion similar to that of a losing boxer in the closing rounds of a fight . . . fists flying in a desperate bid for a win. We had lost patience with caution. It was time to take a gamble.

There was a struggle every week to pay Geoffrey's and Jane's wages. Saturday morning would arrive and I would count the notes and hand them over; and then I would return to Jeannie and say that I envied them as wage-earners. Jeannie and I had aimed at the splendours of individualism without computing what such freedom demands. Personal freedom is a word, not a fact. Personal freedom creates its own chains. We were expanding but the expansion had burdened us with more commitments; expansion was inescapable if we were to keep on Geoffrey and Jane and lift our own lives above those of peasants. We had to spend in order to remain free.

Jane possessed the same wild love for the coast along

which we lived as we did ourselves. It is no ordinary coast. The stretch where Minack lies and where Jane's cottage stood gaunt, staring out at the ocean, is not the kind of country which appeals to the conformist. The splendour of the cliffs does not lead to beaches where people can crowd together, transistors beside them.

The cliffs fall to rocks black and grey where the sea ceaselessly churns, splashing its foam, clutching a rock then releasing it, smothering it suddenly in bad temper, caressing it, slapping it as if in play, sometimes kind with the sun shining on the white ribbon of a wave, a laughing sea throwing spray like confetti, sometimes grey and sullen, then suddenly again a sea of ungovernable fury lashing the cliffs; enraged that for ever and for ever the cliffs look down.

And among the rocks are the pools; some that tempt yet are vicious, beckoning innocently, then in a flash a cauldron of currents; pools that are shallow so that the minnow fish ripple the surface as they dash from view; pools so deep that seaweed looks like a forest far below – inaccessible pools, pools which hide from everyone except those who belong to them.

High above, the little meadows dodge the boulders, and where the land is too rough for cultivation the bracken, the hawthorn, the brambles, the gorse which sparks its yellow the year round, reign supreme. This is no place for interlopers. The walkers, tamed by pavements, faced by the struggling undergrowth, turn back or become angry, their standardised minds piqued that they have to force a way through; and it is left to the few, the odd man or woman, to marvel that there is a corner of England still free from the dead hand of the busybody.

The badgers show the way. Their paths criss-cross, twist, turn, pound the soil flat, a foot wide, high roads of centuries, and when the bracken greens or coppers the land, the way is still there, underneath, so that if you have a feel for the countryside the undergrowth does not halt you. The badgers lead you. As you walk, feet firm and safe, you part the bracken to either side and, after you have passed, it folds back again, leaving no sign of your passage.

Here, on our stretch of the coast, man has not yet brought his conceit. It is as it always has been: gulls sweeping on their way, a buzzard sailing in the sky, foxes safe from the Hunt, birds arriving tired after a long journey, others ready to leave, swallows, whitethroats, chiff-chaffs, fieldfare, snipe, the long list which we welcome and to which we say goodbye. Our stretch of the cliff has a savagery that frightens the faint-hearted.

'Why isn't there a decent path cut along the cliff top? Absolutely disgraceful.'

'All right in the summer, I suppose?'

'I wouldn't live there if it were given to me.'

'How wonderful if uranium was discovered!'

'There's going to be a coastal path. You can't escape it, you know!'

'This is marvellous. An August day in Cornwall and no one to be seen.'

There they are, the philistines and the individual they would like to destroy. Mass enjoyment, mass organised walks, mass anything if it can score a victory over the sensitive; thus the philistines, barren of feeling, plod

their dreary way, earnest, dull, conscientious, honest, misguided – I pity them. So did Jane. But Jane, like ourselves, was infuriated by their conceit.

Every day of our lives was spent in unison with this coast, the rage of the gales, salt smearing our faces as we walked, east winds, south winds, calm summer early morning, the first cubs, a badger in the moonlight, wild violets, the glory of the first daffodil, the blustering madness of making a living on land that faced the roar of the ages. These were the passages of our year. Glorious, hurting, awakening us to the splendour of living. But the philistines. They nose. They want to disturb. Yet they are blind to beauty. They glance at our coast as they rush by. They want to see a path on the map. That is their object. Everything must conform. No time to pause. Hurry, hurry, hurry . . . we have another two miles to go.

The spring came early the following year. In February there were gentle west winds, balmy days which sent the larks into the sky to sing a month before their time. The green woodpecker in the elms below the cottage clung to the bark tapping his note of joy, unperturbed that the splendour of his crimson crown among the bare branches was there for all to see. The sunshine was his safety.

There was a rush of wings in Minack woods. Exultant songs from the willows, blackbirds courting, and thrushes rivalling them with glorious notes. Harsh warbles from the chaffinches, and the trills of the wrens, fluffing their tiny bodies, then bellowing their happiness. Magpies coarsely cried. The two ravens from the cliff flew overhead coughing their comments on what they could see below. Robins were careless in hiding their nests, no time for danger for spring was here. Owls hooted in the daylight. The wintering flocks of starlings gathered in the sky like black confetti wondering whether to leave. Too soon for the chiff-chaffs or the warblers or the whitethroats. They did not know we had an early spring. Minack woods still belonged to those who lived there.

The sea rippled in innocence, and when the *Scillonian* sailed by to and from the Islands we could hear in the cottage the pounding of her engines; for the wind and the surf were silent. Fishermen were tempted to drop their lobster pots, and one of them every day had a string across our tiny bay. There were others feathering for mackerel. Cockleshell-white boats with men in yellow oilskins, engines chattering until the moment came to switch off and to drift with the tide. Gulls aimlessly dotted the water, like lazy holidaymakers. Cormorants on the edge of rocks held out their wings to dry like huge, motionless bats. The first primroses clustered on the cliff's edge and white blooms of blackthorn spattered the wasteland above. A beautiful spring; if only the task was to be part of it but to us it held a threat. There was danger in the lovely days. There was menace in the soft breezes and warm nights. For our livelihood depended on cold. We required brisk weather and frosts up-a-long. How could we sell our flowers if flowers from everywhere were flooding the markets?

I had gone along one morning to open the chickens up when I saw the little black cat inside the run by the chicken-house door. For a second it stared at me, motionless, then it ran, racing across the run in panic, until it hit the wire netting at the far side. Foolishly, I went after it. I do not know what my intentions might have been but my approach increased the cat's terror and it began clawing at the wire and attempting to thrust its head through the mesh. I suddenly realised it might strangle itself. The head might just possibly get through a hole; but its body, thin though it was, never. For an instant I put out my hands as if to pick it up. The threat of such help from me made it instinctively recoil from the netting; and the next moment I saw it take a flying leap on to the chicken-house roof, up the tree, and down again onto the ground outside the run. It disappeared into the wood behind.

Defeat, or danger, is easy to face when it is met suddenly for the first time. One feels elated that the secret self is being challenged. Here is the chance to bring out the hero, the somnolent section of one's being that longs to justify itself in the dramatic. But I always feel that the very nature of the courage that is required on such occasions is deceptive. It looks like courage while in fact it is an emotional outburst. It can be, indeed, a form of showmanship. In times of sudden danger or defeat one can be so intoxicated by excitement that one is scarcely aware of one's actions.

The aftermath of such courage is when real courage is needed. The gesture has been made but the danger has remained, and a hangover has taken the place of exultation. One now slips into a remorseless delaying action, a tedious clinging to hope; and one is forced to realise that factors have to be faced which provide no stimulus. They are the factors of repetition, the further defeats, the further dangers, leading one on and on until suddenly comes the day one discovers that despair has replaced the struggle for victory as the enemy.

This was our first spring at Minack without Monty. His shadow seemed always to be with us. And although when one loses a loved one it is necessary to be practical and not to mope or to be indulgently sentimental, we yearned for the soft fur curled at the bottom of our bed at night, the sudden purrs, the wonderful comfort of his greetings on our returns, the splendour of his person – the colour of autumn bracken – poised ready to pounce on a mouse rustling in the grass.

He had been part of our lives for so long. He had been a friend in the sense that he had always been there to cope with our disappointments, ready to be picked up and hugged or to bring calm with a game or to soothe by sitting on my lap and being gently stroked. He had been an anchor in our life. He was only a cat, but he had shared the years; and thus he would always be part of us.

I said to him on his last day that I would never have another cat. I felt, in saying this, that I was in some strange way repaying his love. I was giving him his identity. I was proving to him that he was not to me just one of a breed who could be replaced, like replacing a broken cup with one of the same pattern. He was Monty, and there would never be another. It would be no use some well-meaning person arriving at the door with a kitten, curbing grief by offering a substitute. I was telling him that I would always be loyal to him. The only cat I had ever known.

And then I made a remark that in retrospect was to prove so extraordinary. I found myself saying that I would make one exception . . . if a black cat whose previous home could never be discovered came crying to the door of the cottage in a storm. I was so astonished by my own words that I went and told Jeannie. I was so ashamed by what I had said. At the very moment I was trying to prove my devotion, I had hedged. I had not meant what I had been saying to Monty. My emotion had deceived me and my subconscious had come out with the truth. I would, in fact, accept a successor. True, I was able to console myself by realising I had made an apparently impossible condition.

A tremendous storm was blowing and as I often do when this happens, I switched on the trawler waveband to hear what the ships thought of the weather. The unknown voices came over the air from ships I would never know, and yet so frank, so intimate were these voices that I felt I could have taken part in their conversations. Suddenly I heard a cry at the door.

'Did you hear that, Jeannie?'

One can imagine cries in a storm, or cars arriving, or planes overhead. When the gales blow I am always saying that I hear someone shouting, or Jeannie believes someone has roared down the lane in his car, or I am imagining an airline in trouble. This is what happens when you live in isolation and there are no standardised sounds of civilisation to measure against unreality.

'I thought it was a miaow,' said Jeannie.

And it was.

I opened the door and there was the little black cat huddled outside in the rain. It did not wait for me to invite it in. It rushed past my feet into the room, and sat itself down at the foot of the bookshelf which hides the sink; and waited there, as Monty had always done, yellow eyes looking up at Jeannie for the saucer she was only too ready to give it.

What was I to do? It had acted according to plan. It had fulfilled the conditions. I had put up a resistance, as indeed I had done when Monty was produced to me at the Savoy as a kitten, but the situation was beyond my control. How could I deny a home to a cat which had come to Minack in such a remarkable way?

She is still with us today, three years later, and she is over there now curled up in the corner of the sofa, plump and as glossy as a ripe blackberry. I cannot believe she is the same little black cat which hurled itself against the wire netting of the chicken run.

And her name? She is called Lama, after the Dalai Lama who was at the time escaping from Tibet.

One afternoon, an afternoon when we had a particularly good crop of potatoes, Jeannie came calling for me in anguish.

'Hubert's been shot . . . been *shot*.'

I found Hubert on the cedar-wood top of the coal shed where Jeannie always fed him. He was standing on one leg. The other was hanging limply, and blood covered the webbing of the foot. Every few seconds he staggered, hopping an inch or two, his wings unfurling and flapping, trying to keep his balance. He still looked as regal as ever, and he was glaring at us as if he were in the mood of one who was cursing himself for the mess he was in, like an old man who had at last lost his independence.

'What have you done, old chap?' I asked. 'What happened?'

'He's been shot, I tell you,' Jeannie answered for him angrily. 'I was standing here when he came down and I saw quite clearly a bullet hole through the webbing of his foot.'

Hubert never came again. A gale blew up that night and raged across the sea from the south, surging the waves on the rocks where Hubert used to shelter, tearing with the sound of tube trains round the cottage, doom in the noise, so that Jeannie and I lay awake talking and wondering and afraid; and in the morning the gale still blew, and it was so fierce that even if Hubert had been well he would have stayed away from the cottage. He always used to stay away in a storm; and then, when we saw him again, swooping down from the sky to perch on the roof, we used to say a prayer of thanks. Rage had been expended, peace had returned. Normality had replaced cruelty.

Shelagh was working for us now. They were lucky, she and Jane, in that they both had a feel for flowers, and a love of the earth, and a communion with blazing suns and roaring winds; and they had minds which found excitement in small things, the sight of a bird they could not identify, or an insect, or a wild plant they had found in the wood. They were always on the edge of laughter, of pagan intuition, of generosity of spirit. They were not cursed by the sense of meanness, of jealousy of others, of defiance. They wanted to love. There was so much in life to be exultant about and I never knew either of them, even in fun, say a harsh thing about anyone.

Both of them were secretive and why not? It is impertinence, I think, for those with experience to question the young. The young are a race apart with magical values and standards, with mysterious frustrations and victories, free from repeated defeats, fresh, maturing, bouncing into danger, propelled by opposites, frightened, confused by what is told them. And their lecturers, I believe, are those who, having failed in their conduct of their own lives, recoil to the hopes of their youth, reliving ambitions by pontificating, hurting the sensitive young and being laughed at by the others. Experience should be listened to by the young. It should never be inflicted on them.

Both of them had the same stature, Jane, like Shelagh, had the mind which instinctively helped the helpless. Here were these two at Minack, sustaining Jeannie and me with the glory of enthusiasm. In this place we loved so much were these two who shared the pleasures we, so much older, felt ourselves. The young voices calling for their hopes amongst the gales and the rain and the heat. So far to go. So passionately willing to give the present.

Jane was always more sure of herself than Shelagh because she had been loved for herself, since she could remember. And yet, in her way, Jane was as vulnerable. She loved the weak; but when she demonstrated this love she liked to dispense an atmosphere of drama. It was fun to do so. And so it was in this mood she arrived at her work one summer's morning and disclosed an exciting piece of news.

'Mr Tangye,' she said breathlessly, 'a Muscovy drake spent the night in my bedroom. We want to find a home for him. Can he come to you?'

The Muscovy drake had arrived in a sack brought in the back of a car by a young farmer who aimed to make himself popular with the Wyllie family. He could not have created a worse impression. Jane, Jeremy and their mother would have starved rather than eat it.

It was magnificent. It was a large white bird, the size of a goose, with dark green feathers on its back, a powerful pink beak with a red bobble on it bridged by two holes like nostrils, huge yellow webbed feet, an angry red skin beneath the white feathers of its neck and head, piercing, intelligent eyes, and the ability to raise the crest of feathers on its head when annoyed, like the fur of a furious cat. It could also hiss like a steam engine.

Jane brought it across the fields from her cottage, in her arms, unperturbed by its apparent ferocity, and she arrived at our door as if she were holding a Ming vase. I looked at it apprehensively.

'And what, Jane,' I asked, 'is the procedure for looking after a Muscovy drake?'

Julius was one of those sixteen-year-olds who seem to mature before their time. He was on holiday from his school in Switzerland and staying not far away. We had known him off and on since he was a child, and one day this particular summer he had suddenly appeared at the cottage. He was good looking, erudite even for an adult, and effortless as far as Jeannie and I were concerned. He had a restless wish to be alone on the cliff, and he would come to us, have a meal and then go off down to the rocks by himself; and later I would find him there staring out to sea.

'What are you thinking about, Julius?'

And in reply I would have a penetrating commentary on world affairs, or a more personal outlook on life. One did not think of him as younger than oneself. One had with him a standard of conversation like playing tennis on the centre court at Wimbledon. The ideas bounced back at one another with speed.

As soon as he found the tin bath he dug a hole in the chicken run, the exact size, so the rim of the bath was on a level with the surrounding soil; and then he carried water to it until it was filled. We waited expectantly for the drake's reaction and in due course he waddled towards it, dipped his beak into the water, and a minute later was sitting in it looking like a battleship in a small lagoon. 'Well done, Boris,' said Julius.

'Why Boris?' asked Jeannie.

'Well, he must have a name and as he is a Muscovy he ought to have a name which sounds like a Russian.'

I envy those who are able to treat pets casually as if

they exist only to titillate man's boredom. I envy them their harshness. They can pursue their relationship with birds and animals on a metallic basis, a scientist's standard. Emotion in their eyes is a vulgar thing. They do not suffer as the rest of us suffer. The heart of a bird or an animal does not exist and so they can treat them like a new toy, gloriously loved on its arrival then simmering into being a nuisance, then back again at intervals to being loved again.

Love for an animal is no less than love for a human being. It is indeed more vulnerable. One can console oneself by the assurance that a human being can evict disillusion by contact with his friends. But an animal yields trust with the abandon of a child and if it is betrayed, shoved here and there, treated as baggage or merchandise, bargained over like a slave of olden days, everyone except the cynic can understand the hurt in its eyes. But the cynic grouses that we who see this hurt are suffering from a surfeit of sentiment, the word which the cynic parades so often as if it were his fortress.

Sometimes on these summer mornings when the Jackson order was a big one, Shelagh would come in early too. And there were occasions when Julius would also arrive proudly.

'A record walk this morning. Clipped a minute off my time.'

His was a wonderful walk. He was sleeping in a caravan in the woods of an estate a couple of miles away; and the route to Minack was across green fields that were raised like a plateau above the sea, then down into a valley where a stream rushed in haste, leaping the boulders, sheltered by a wood where foxes hid, bordered by lush vegetation in summer, and in winter welcoming snipe and woodcock giving them a home safe from the guns. Julius loved this walk. He crossed the valley, then up past Jane's cottage and over the stone hedges to Minack.

'Heavens, Julius, I didn't expect to see you today.'

'I thought I might be able to help.'

He would always quickly go and have a look at Boris because, I believe, he was proud that he had named him. There was, for always, a link between the two. It may not have been very important, but then I sometimes wonder how to gauge the degrees of importance. I have remembered many things, which at the time outsiders would have considered insignificant.

Julius was one of those people who, youthful though they may be, instinctively wish to help others. It is not just the question of practical help. It is the art of conversation, or of silence; the intuition when to continue a line of thought, or when to stop. There are no lessons to be given about these things; the sense of embarrassment which for a second may be hinted, or the flicker in eyes which gives a clue to secret hurt, or the flavour of a moment which insists on a change of subject, none of these occasions can be dealt with by rule of thumb. Instinct is the king.

Thus Jeannie and I would be there with these three who had the promise of the years before them, each helping us, each so full of secret thoughts and hopes, puzzled, contradictory, timid and brave, obstinate and imaginative. I understood why Jeannie said to me one day that she was grateful for the necessity of cutting lettuces; a humble task, perhaps, but there was more to gain than the price received.

The promise of the years ... how strange it was, in view of what was to happen, that it should be Shelagh, living now in the same caravan a year later, who told us that Julius had died in a motor accident.

It was fortunate that shortly afterwards A. P. Herbert came to stay with us. It was particularly fortunate as far as Shelagh was concerned because A. P. H. was co-operating with Russ Conway, who was writing the music, on a version of *A Christmas Carol*. The looks, character, and personality of Russ Conway provided Shelagh with an ideal. He could do no wrong. He provided her with all the sweetness of a first love without the heartbreaks of reality. A photograph, scissored from a magazine, was in her caravan. The only picture of a star she had. And now here was someone actually staying with us who was in regular contact with him.

We did not tell Shelagh what we planned. And when the envelope arrived addressed to her in which, we knew, was a personal letter from Russ Conway and a signed photograph, we handed it to her as casually as if it were a circular.

Half an hour later I called into the flower-house where she was having her lunch. She was sitting with Lama on her lap, the photograph propped against a jam jar beside her, a sandwich in one hand, the letter in the other.

I did not have to ask her whether she was pleased.

Nor did she have to say anything. She had the smile of the happiest girl in the world.

I do not believe age determines whether or not you can be on the same wavelength as another. There is simply a meeting of minds of whatever age which instantly feel at ease, just as there are other times when people, hard as they may try to prevent it, find they resent each other, or are bored. Thus a child can find that his thoughts are fluent, so too the means to express them with one teacher, while an hour later, in another class, he finds himself dumb. It is simply that he has been with one teacher who was on his wavelength, another who was not.

Jane won the Prince of Wales Cup, the youngest competitor ever to do so.

As for ourselves, we were bewildered by the strain and the success. We were all very quiet. I remember coming into the cottage and saying to Jane what a wonderful experience it had been for Jeannie and me that the schoolgirl who had once called on us for a job had won such a victory. The sound of the storm was still in my ears. I was still dazed.

Then suddenly I heard Jane's soft voice; and what she said brought to the surface why, in fact, we were so quiet.

'How Shelagh would have loved these past two days!'

Jane was sitting on the same chair where she sat the day she first came to Minack, Jeannie was sitting opposite her on the sofa. I picked up a pipe from my desk and began to fill it.

'A year ago she was celebrating her prize for bunched violets. She was so pleased with that win,' I said.

There was silence for a moment. Then I said: 'She didn't suffer. She was unconscious even when she fell off her bicycle. When she was a child she had been in hospital with heart trouble.'

'She never showed any signs that anything was wrong while I was with her.'

'None of us had any warning.'

Jeannie was stroking Lama who had jumped on her lap.

'You were great friends, Jane,' she said, 'I will always remember you together.'

'Oh yes. She was coming to stay with us on Tresco last Easter, the week she died.'

Jeannie turned to her; and at this instant I found myself seeing again Shelagh's delicious smile when she was very happy.

'Just think, Jane,' Jeannie said, 'how glad she would be for you today.'

A Donkey in the Meadow

*There they were, two donkeys with ice-cream smeared
about their faces, sucking lollipops; Fred a toy donkey,
Penny a working one, when the time came for The Cake,
Jeannie had made it, a table on the field was ready for
it, and there was a single candle.*

We had bought our tickets to Paddington. We had
decided to stay at the Savoy, the first time together there
since Jeannie had written *Meet Me at the Savoy*. We
both had a pleasant sense of anticipation of the happy
time ahead. It was Friday and we were going to leave
by the Sunday night train. Everything, in fact, about the

holiday was organized, when the Lamorna post master strode down the lane with a telegram. The message said simply: 'Got Donkey. Teague.'

I looked at the telegram in dismay.

'Heavens, Jeannie,' I said, 'now what do we do?'

Mr Teague, a Dickensian toby jug of a man, kept the Plume of Feathers at Scorrier, near Redruth. He was also a cattle dealer, a horse dealer, a dealer in any kind of animal. We had had a drink with him a couple of weeks previously.

'I never said definitely I wanted one,' she murmured. 'I only talked to him about it. I never thought he had taken me seriously.'

I glanced at her suspiciously.

'You promise you didn't make some secret plan with him? . . . arrange for him to produce a donkey just as you arranged with your mother to give us Monty? . . . presenting me with a *fait accompli*?'

'Don't be silly.'

'You've always been so dotty about donkeys that I could believe anything.'

Jack Baker was a landscape gardener, and at this time was designing a new part of our garden. He was a practical man, an expert horticulturalist, a mechanic, a tree-feller and, what interested me particularly, he had had experience with donkeys.

'Tell me, Jack,' I said when I found him, 'what do you think about keeping a donkey as a pet?'

Jack had a merry eye but a lugubrious nature. He wanted to enjoy life but the fates had checked him so many times that he was inclined always to outline the tedious side of a problem at the expense of the happier side. He was in his fifties, tall and broad-shouldered, an individualist who, during the war, preferred to remain a sergeant in the Guards rather than accept the commission he was offered. He was one of those rare people one would instinctively want to be with in a jam. He would, I felt sure, be calm while the threat – whatever it was – received his attention. I anxiously awaited his donkey views.

He took the pipe from his mouth, knocked the ash from the bowl on a rock, then pronounced:

'You'll have a packet of trouble.'

I was, of course, prepared for a douche of cold water. He was only being true to my knowledge of him, a harbinger of bad news before good; and yet his attitude, because it coincided with my own, was pleasing to listen to.

'How do you mean?' I asked.

'Well, the first thing you'll find out, for instance,' he said solemnly, 'is that it will eat up the garden.'

Even to my ears this remark sounded biased. What about a horse or a cow? Wouldn't they eat up the garden if they were given a chance?

Jack was leaning on his shovel, amused, delighting in his mission to discomfort me.

'Ah,' he said knowingly. 'A horse or a cow can be kept in a field and it's only bad luck if it gets out. But a donkey! You can't keep a donkey loose in a field. It'll get out. It'll jump a fence or a wall, and go roaming all over the district. And it'll be eating up other people's gardens besides yours.'

'What do people do about donkeys then?'

He grinned at me.

'Best thing to do is to tether it. You get a swivel anchor from the blacksmith, fix it firmly in the ground, and the donkey goes round and round eating the grass. Then twice a day you move it.'

'Twice a day?'

'Oh yes, otherwise as soon as it has eaten the grass it will start braying.'

'It's a bit of a job digging up the anchor and then fixing it again, isn't it?'

'Certainly. But that's what people do.'

I could not see myself doing it.

'There's another point,' Jack went on, and he was now talking as if he believed he had got me on the run, 'and that's water. A donkey drinks a lot and you'll have to keep a bucket always full beside it. If a donkey is thirsty even for a minute the braying will start up.'

'How loud is the braying?'

'They'll hear it in the next parish.'

'But surely,' I said, 'you're exaggerating. You're making out that a donkey is only fit for a zoo. After all, lots of people do keep donkeys.'

'Not for long. They're excited when they get them at first but soon tire of them when they find out the trouble they cause.'

I found at this moment, contrary to reason, that Jack's attitude was engaging my sympathy for donkeys. His arguments against them seemed, even to me, to be overloaded.

'Now tell me honestly,' I said, 'how friendly can a donkey be?'

He sat down on a rock, put his palms on his knees, laughingly looked at me with his head on one side, and replied:

'How friendly? You ask me how friendly? . . . all I can say is I would never dare keep a donkey myself!'

We reached the Plume of Feathers soon after opening time, and Mr Teague greeted us with a glint in his eye. He saw a sale in the offing.

'Come in,' he said jovially from behind the bar, 'have a drink. What'll you have, Mrs Tangye?'

Mr Teague, or Roy as he now insisted on us calling him, was in the fortunate position of being able to do his bargaining on his own licensed premises. Sales could be conducted in convivial circumstances, and though a purchaser might succeed in reducing a price or a seller in increasing it, the cost of the evening had to be considered. I was aware of this. I had therefore decided, in the event of us wishing to buy the donkey, to complete the deal with the minimum of argument. I might lose a pound or two on the price, but this was a sensible sacrifice if it meant we could speedily return to Minack.

'We've just looked in to see the donkey,' I said casually. 'It was very nice of you to send the telegram.'

'Not at all,' he said. 'I've got a nice little donkey and thought I'd let you have the first chance.'

He had got us our drinks and was now leaning with elbows on the bar, hands interlocked. I could see he was about to turn his charm on Jeannie. She was a vulnerable target.

'Lovely-tempered little donkey,' he said, smiling at

her, 'good as gold. Comes from Ireland, from Connemara or somewhere like that. They ship them over by the dozen these days.'

'What for?'

'They go for pet food mostly.'

'How cruel,' said Jeannie.

He was now fiddling with an empty ash tray on the counter.

'The only trouble is she is not in very good condition. Nothing serious. Nothing that Dr Green can't soon put right.'

'Dr Green?' I asked, puzzled.

'Grass.'

'Oh, of course.'

He turned again to Jeannie. His eyes were twinkling.

'And there's another thing. Something, I bet, you never bargained for when you came along here. She's in foal. Two donkeys for one. What about that?'

I took a gulp at my drink.

'Good heavens!' I said.

'Now, now, now,' he answered, looking at me and sensing a momentary set-back, 'as soon as she's had the foal I'll buy it off you. Nothing could be fairer than that, could it?'

He turned again to Jeannie.

'Have you ever seen a little donkey foal? Lovely little things they are. Just like a toy. You can pick it up in your arms. I've seen a child do that, honestly I have.'

I watched Jeannie melting. The practical side, the prospect of two donkeys charging about Minack did not concern her at all. All that she could imagine was the picture card idyll of a donkey and its foal. The deal was advancing in his favour. Somewhere in a field behind the pub was a donkey which was on the brink of being ours.

And then Mr Teague played his ace.

'Sad thing about this donkey,' he said, fumbling again with the ash tray, 'very sad thing ... By the way, Penny's her name. Pretty name Penny, isn't it?'

'You were saying.'

'Yes, I was going to tell you that if you don't like the look of her, I've got a buyer. Made a good offer he has too, but it's a sad story.'

'Why so sad?'

'Well, I wouldn't like to see it happen. You see the idea of this buyer is to wait for the foal to be born, then put it in a circus. A donkey foal in a circus would be a big draw, especially on the holiday circuit. Can't you see the children flocking round it?'

I could see he was genuinely concerned.

'What happens to the mother?'

He glanced at me, appreciating that I was on the wavelength.

'That's the point. That's what I'm worried about. That's why I want to find her a good home, and thought of you two.'

'How do you mean?'

'The idea of this buyer friend of mine is to send Penny to the knacker's yard as soon as the youngster can get along without her.'

'But that's awful.' I could not help myself from saying what I knew was in Jeannie's mind.

'And what's more,' went on Roy Teague, 'when the season is over and they've got their money's worth out of the youngster, it'll be too big to keep.' He paused. 'They'll send it to the knacker's yard as well.'

Rain began to spatter the windscreen as we turned from the main road into the bumpy lane which led a mile away to Minack. Clouds, low and lugubrious, swirling in from the sea and the south, were hastening the dusk to fall before its time.

'I feel very pleased with myself,' said Jeannie suddenly.

'Why's that?'

'Well,' she said, 'before we left and when you were out of sight, I got hold of Jack Baker and asked him a favour.'

'And what was this favour?'

'It was his idea really.'

'Come on, tell me what it was.'

I felt irked that I had not been previously informed.

'You know that big iron bar which is used for levering rocks?'

'Of course I do.'

'Jack Baker suggested it would make an ideal tethering post for a donkey.'

'Reasonable enough.'

'And so before we set off just in case we *did* buy a donkey, I asked him to fix it.'

'You seemed very certain in that case that we *would* buy a donkey.'

'The only trouble is,' she said, ignoring me, 'that he couldn't put it upright and the soil was too shallow. He therefore planned to anchor it into the ground horizontally, helped by a couple of big rocks at either end of the bar.'

A journey into detail was unlike Jeannie. She was hiding something.

'The bar,' she went on, 'is all in except where the rope is tied. The other end of the rope we join to the halter we've brought with us. It means that Penny can't run away.'

We passed the jumble of farm buildings which stood at the top of the valley, then began to descend the last stretch to the cottage. And all the time Penny's head rested firmly on my shoulder.

'Whereabouts,' I asked, 'am I going to find this contraption?'

'On the lawn.'

I calmed myself. I kept my hands on the wheel. I said nothing.

'I know what you're thinking,' she went on, 'I can guess. But . . . honestly, it isn't much of a lawn. Now is it?'

'Hell,' I said, 'it's started to pour.'

I drew up outside the cottage and as I did so I saw the rain dancing on the bonnet; and when I switched off the engine I could hear the wind sweeping through the elm trees.

'It's going to be a dirty old night.'

'What a beginning for her.'

'She's got to get used to it some time. And, anyhow, didn't she come from Ireland?'

'That doesn't mean she enjoys rough weather.'

'Nor do we. And we are about to be soaked trying to lure a donkey from the back of a Land-rover towards

THE WORLD OF MINACK

a contraption outside our bedroom window, and keeping it from running away.'

'Come on, Penny,' I said, gently pulling the rope of the halter, 'turn round.'

She stayed staring across the front seats at the windscreen.

'Do please turn round.'

I pulled again, firmly this time. It was like pulling a tree trunk.

'For heaven's sake, Penny, *turn round*.'

No response.

'I'll get a carrot,' said Jeannie, running indoors and returning with a handful.

'Look, Penny,' I said, tugging at her again and holding a carrot like a flag, 'look what I've got.'

I awoke soon after dawn and I lay there sleepily, listening to the dawn chorus, attempting to identify the many songs. The storm had passed and it was still again; and through the window I could see the crescent of the sun climbing behind the Lizard. It was a heavenly morning, and for a brief moment I believed I possessed no cares. Then suddenly I realised why I had woken so early.

There, just outside the bedroom window, was a donkey. A responsibility. I had waited for years for a holiday and I had sacrificed it to a four-legged creature which would be useless for any practical purpose. There would be nothing for it to do except mooch about demanding attention. And soon there would be a foal. Two donkeys mooching about.

They would live for years and years; and every day

I would be waking up, half worrying what to do with them. Should they be in this meadow, or that? Have they got enough water? We had burdened ourselves with two large permanent pets, remote in manner but utterly dependent upon us. I had been rushed into making a purchase that any cool period of thinking would have made me check, see reason, and halt from making. On this lovely, fresh early morning I was angry with myself.

Lama's attitude was one of benign approval from her first sight of Penny. One might have expected upright fur and an arched back, a mood of anger or terror, when Penny like a moving mountain advanced towards her, a black cat so small that some people still mistook her for a kitten. Not a bit of it. There was not a quiver of a whisker nor a twitch of the tail. She was serenely confident that Penny threatened no harm.

This belief of Lama that nothing, not even a motor car, possessed any evil intentions towards her, frequently caused us alarm. How was it possible that the character of a cat could so change? Only three years before she was wild, and now nothing scared her. If a car came down the lane she lay in the middle until the car had to stop. If a dog lunged from a lead and barked insults, she complacently stared back, a Gandhi policy of non-violence. If a cat hater tried to avoid her, she pursued him with purrs. Once I saw a fox cub taking a look at her from a few yards off as she lay, a miniature Trafalgar lion, in the grass. When she became aware of his attention she got up, stretched and walked peacefully towards him. What does one do with a cat so trusting?

It is a sickness of the mid-twentieth century that the basic virtues are publicised as dull. The arbiters of this age, finding it profitable to destroy, decree from the heights that love and trust and loyalty are suspect qualities; and to sneer and be vicious, to attack anyone or any cause which possesses roots, to laugh at those who cannot defend themselves, are the aims to pursue. Their ideas permeate those who only look but do not think. Jokes and debating points, however unfair, are hailed as fine entertainment. Truth, by this means, becomes unfashionable.

Guerrilla warfare continues ceaselessly between those who love animals and those who believe the loving is grossly overdone. Animals, in some people's view, can contribute nothing to the brittle future of our computer civilisation, and therefore to love them or to care for them is a decadent act. Other people consider that in a world in which individualism is a declining status, an animal reflects their own wish to be free. These people also love an animal for its loyalty. They sometimes feel that their fellow human beings are so absorbed by their self survival that loyalty is considered a liability in the pursuit of material ambition. Animals, on the other hand, can bestow dependable affection and loyalty on all those who wish to receive it.

'I have a feeling,' said Jeannie's mother later, 'that this donkey is going to be a nuisance!'

She did not, of course, mean this to be a reproach. Nor for that matter a warning. It was a gentle joke, said in a soft voice with just the trace of a Scottish accent. I realise in retrospect that her affection for Fred, the foal, stemmed from something deeper than superficial enchantment for a Disney-like creature. He was to her, in the last few months of her life, a link with the future. Her intuition made her aware that time was against her, and so she was glad to find in this absurd little donkey a bridge. Jeannie's uncle told Jeannie how a few weeks later he was with her mother waiting for a bus to take them from Gloucester Road to Hyde Park corner. They waited twenty minutes at the bus stop, not because there were no buses. Three went by; but Jeannie's mother went on talking, and the subject was Fred. The poor man cursed the donkey as he stood there, listening patiently. He did not know the secret. Fred, at that very instant, running free on the Cornish cliffs, the skies and wild winds, sunny days and torrential rain, the sea lurching then calm, scents of the salt, wild grasses, pinks, meadowsweet, puzzling cries of gulls, woodpeckers laughing, badgers solidly plodding ageless paths, foxes alert, exultant chorus of the early morning, marsh warblers, summer larks, blackbirds trumpeting, wrens erupting; for all these Fred was the spokesman. These pleasures, enriched by the eyes and ears of centuries, projecting the kindness of permanence and security, dwelt there hopefully in her mind.

A month after she had returned to London, and Jeannie was with her. I took a pair of scissors and cut a

small piece of Fred's mane and sent it to her tied with a pale blue ribbon. It was still in her handbag eight months later when she died.

'Whatever else he does in his life,' said Jeannie thoughtfully, 'Fred has justified his existence.'

Fred now faced a glorious summer of adulation. Nobody could resist him. Children and grown-ups both uttered cries of delight as soon as they saw his gambolling fluffy figure. Cameras were poised, small hands held out to stroke him, picnic baskets searched for sugar; and his response was to pander to his admirers in various fetching ways. Sometimes he would stand beside them staring soulfully into the distance as they stroked him, sometimes he would surprise a new admirer by a comical harmless dance, sometimes he would show off his speed by sprinting across the meadow, sometimes he would hug close to Penny, but always, sooner or later, he would allow every admirer to fondle him.

An eloquent feature of the donkeys was their stare; and we never succeeded in growing accustomed to it. It was a weapon they used in morose moments of displeasure. There they would stand, side by side in a meadow, steadfastly watching us, exuding disapproval, condemning us for going about our business and not theirs.

The stare increased in its frequency after the summer and the visitors had disappeared; for Fred, by this time, expected attention like a precocious child film star who believes that adulation goes on for ever. He missed the applause, lumps of sugar, and posing for his picture. He was a prince without courtiers. He was at a loss as to how to fill his day. So he would stare, and hope that we would fill the gap.

One October night, a still, unusually warm night of dense fog, the watchfulness of the donkeys was challenged by an event of great drama. We had left them down in the cliff meadows and this in itself was an adventure for them. They loved these meadows. Not only was there a profusion of their favourite grasses in various stages of growth, but there were also the evergreen privet and escallonia. I had taken them there many times during the daytime but this was the first occasion they had been allowed to stay for the night; and I had done so because when at nightfall I had called them from the gate to come up, they had not taken the slightest notice. The meadows were steep, pocket-size meadows intertwining one into the other, cascading like stepping stones downwards to the rocks and the sea. Once I used many of them for early potatoes, heaving the sacks up the cliff path; but now they were our daffodil meadows, and in January and February they danced with yellow, the splash of the waves on rocks their orchestra. As yet, in October, not even the spikes of green had appeared; and we even, flatteringly, praised the donkeys for being useful. They at least were helping towards keeping the grass trimmed.

I will always wonder whether they were frightened by what happened. Did Fred, more highly strung than Penny, begin immediately to hee-haw? And was he heard by any of the men hanging on to the driftwood? It seems certain that he was. And did Penny join in, so that the two of them tolled for the doomed? I can see them in my mind, ears upright like Churchill's victory sign, keen eyes blind in the darkness, noses quivering, listening to the mysterious noises, useless sentinels of disaster.

I saw through the window a hatless elderly man come puffing up the path from the direction of the field, followed a moment later by a formidable-looking lady. I dashed out of the cottage to meet them, sensing immediately that something had gone awry.

'Can I help you?' I said, using my usual method of introduction, smiling politely, and at the same time wondering what on earth had happened to cause such obvious excitement.

'Are those your damned donkeys in the field we've just come through?' barked the man. He was out of breath as if he had been running and as he spoke he mopped his bald head with a handkerchief.

'Yes,' I replied doubtfully. 'Anything wrong?'

'Very much so,' interrupted the lady, grimly, looking at me from under an old felt hat. 'The young one snatched my husband's cap and is running round the field with it.'

How had Fred managed it? Had he sneaked up behind the couple as they hurried along, annoyed they had taken no notice of him, and then performed a ballet dancer's leap to take the cap from the gentleman's head?

'Good gracious,' I said, 'I do apologise for this. I'll go ahead straight away and catch him.'

I ran away from them laughing, down the path to the field, asking myself what I would have to do if Fred had gobbled it up. But as I did so I suddenly saw a galloping Fred coming towards me, tweed cap in mouth, and just behind him a thundering, rollocking Penny; and the two of them gave such an impression of joyous, hilarious elation that I only wished that Jeannie had been with me to see them.

The cap was intact, a little wet, but no sign of a tear; and when I thankfully returned it to its owner I asked what had happened. It was simple. It was almost as I imagined it. The couple had sat down on the grass for a rest; and then up behind them came Fred. And away went the cap.

Fred met his first winter and viewed it with apprehension. No one to visit him. No flavour in the grass. Hedgerows bare. Long nights with nothing to do. Driving rain to flatten his fluffy coat. And gales.

How he hated gales. Rain, however heavy, was only an inconvenience by comparison. He would stand in the rain hour after hour, spurning the welcoming open door of the stables, looking miserable nevertheless, taking apparently some kind of masochistic pleasure out of his discomfort. I was sorry for him in the rain but I did not feel I was under any obligation to take steps to protect him from it. A really persistent long day's rain would put him in a stupor, and if I called him he would pause a moment or two before lifting his head dazedly to look at me. He seldom showed any wish to come to me; he and Penny, heads down, the rain dripping off their noses, bottoms towards the weather, would stand stoically content in what I would have thought were intolerable conditions.

But in gales he needed protection. He became restless as soon as the first breeze, the scout of the gale, began hurrying across the field; and he would begin to hee-haw, lifting his head to the scurrying clouds so that a mournful bellow joined the swish of the wind in the trees. He would not stand still, but would race round in small circles, then dash off to another part of the field; and instead of following Penny dutifully about as was his usual custom, Penny would be hastening after him. He was the leader. It was as if he believed that something tangible was chasing him, not a gale but an enemy with plans to capture him. A foolish fantasy of the very young, faced by the unknown.

Penny herself, with private memories of the Connemara mountains, was unperturbed. She felt, no doubt, that Fred's fears were part of his education, and that repetition would dull them. She plodded after him as he ran hither and thither like an old nanny after a child, and when he grew tired she would nudge him along to the shelter of a hedge. Penny was very weather-wise. She had mapped each meadow with a number of tactical positions to suit every variation of the wind; a series of well worn patches on the ground disclosed them. Thus, if a westerly moved a few points to the east resulting in her current position being exposed, she cunningly led the way to the next patch.

On Christmas Eve we took mince pies to the donkeys in the stable. A lighthearted gesture, a game for ourselves, an original diet for them.

'Donkeys! Donkeys!' Jeannie called into the darkness of the meadow. 'Come into the stable. We've got something for you.' And after a minute or two, their shadows loomed, heralded by inquiring whimpers.

'Fred,' I said, 'you're about to have your first mince pie.'

Inside we lit a candle, in an old-fashioned candlestick, and put it on the window sill. The light flickered softly. It flickered on their white noses, their eager faces, their giant rabbit-like ears. They pushed their heads forward, nuzzling us in expectation.

'Patience, patience!' said Jeannie, holding the mince pies high in her hand, 'don't be in such a hurry!' And then with a quick movement she gave one to each of them.

As I stood watching I began to feel the magic of the occasion. Our intention had been to have a joke, to enjoy the merry spirit of Christmas and now, unexpectedly, something else was taking place.

'Look at their crosses,' I said to Jeannie. The cross of Penny was black merging into black, but that of Fred was easy to see; the dark line tracing up the backbone beneath his fluffy brown coat until it reached his shoulders, then stopping abruptly when it met the two lines tracing down each foreleg. 'Here we are,' I went on, 'with two biblical creatures eating mince pies.'

'In a stable.'

'On Christmas Eve.'

There was the gentle sound as they shifted their feet on the cobblestones, and I was aware of the musty scent of their coats. Ageless simplicity, laughed at, beaten, obstinately maintaining an individuality; here indeed was a moment when there was a communication with the past. Struggle, self-sacrifice, integrity, loyalty; how was it that the basic virtues, the proven talisman of man's true happiness, were being lost in the rush of material progress? Why was it that civilisation was allowing its soul to be destroyed by brain power and the vacuous desire it breeds? Why deify the automaton when selflessness has to be won? For a shimmering moment we felt the race halted. No contrived, second-hand emotion. We were not watching, we were part. As it always had been, so it was now.

Jeannie and I had the home but we were, on the other hand, disorganised. I sometimes felt I behaved like a rabbit caught in the glare of headlights dashing this way and that without purpose until it zigzags its way to the safety of a burrow. I seemed incapable of solving the problems around me. I would have one idea, then another, then another, and none of them would ever quite come off. I was safe at Minack but I was not progressing. My imagination became congealed, for instance, by the tedious detail of spending three days, Jeannie beside me, on my hands and knees weeding freesias; and we would both become doped by the simplicity of the task. We would cheer when we had finished. We would gaze in admiration at the neat beds and convince ourselves that something worthwhile had been achieved. So it had been. Unhappily it was at the price of thinking. There is a soothing, narcotic daziness in weeding which pleasingly seduces you from concentrating on plans for the future. A day of weeding might satisfy our consciences but it did not advance us. It only helped to obscure the trouble we were in.

The shadows fall early on our cliff. The setting sun is still comparatively high behind the hill when the rocks begin to point their fingers towards the sea. It becomes cool when on the top of the hill it is still warm. You soon have a sense of impending sleep, a settling for the night as the confetti of gulls drift against the dying sky, floating to smooth rocks, calling from time to time. I would then carry the baskets we had filled up the steep path to the field, load them into the Land-rover, and the two of us would drive up the field and along the track to Minack. The same track, the same view awaiting us, as when years before, at a moment of despair, we looked ahead of us, and Jeannie called out as if our problems had been solved: 'Look! There's a gull on the roof!'

I was up early on the morning of Fred's birthday, a glorious hazy, warm May morning, and went down to the rocks for a bathe. Fishing boats, half a mile offshore, were hurrying to Newlyn market and gulls swirled in their wake. Two cormorants on the other side of the little bay, black sentinels in the sunlight, were standing on a rock regally surveying the scene; and on my left, up in the woods of the cliff, wood pigeons cooed. The scent of the sea filled the air, crystals sparkled the water, and the sound of the lazy, lapping waves was like a chorus of ghosts telling the world to hush. No angry engines in the sky disturbed the peace of it. No roar of traffic dulled the senses. Here was the original freedom. Here was poised a fragment of time when the world was young.

When I returned to the cottage, Fred and Penny were standing in the field looking down into the garden, and Jeannie was at the door.

'We've been waiting for you,' she said, laughing, 'Fred's been getting impatient.'

He began to whimper, nostrils quivering, the prelude to a bellow. 'Hold it, Fred, hold it,' I called, 'we've got a present for you!' Then Jeannie went inside and brought back a huge bunch of carrots. 'Happy birth-day!' we said, holding them in front of him.

Fred, and Penny for that matter, was clearly surprised at such an array of carrots so early in the morning. They were even more surprised when ten minutes later two children's voices came singing round the corner: 'Happy birthday to you!' Susan and Janet from the farm at the top had arrived, like Cornish pixies, with their presents. More carrots! And it was not yet eight o'clock.

I heard the postman singing his way down the lane on his bicycle. Part-time postman, cobbler, hairdresser, fish and chip merchant, he had a key part to play in the coming events. He also sold ice-creams. And he always arrived at Minack happily smiling, whatever the gales, the rain or the snow.

'Lovely morning, Mr Gilbert,' I said.

'And a lovely morning for a donkey's birthday,' he replied. He began to search through his satchel. 'I've got something here I've never carried before. A telegram for a donkey! And there's a big envelope for Fred too. Birthday cards from the school.' He paused, still searching. 'Ah, here they are . . .' Then he added when he handed them to me: 'I've seen the schoolmaster. Thirty-two will be coming from the school, and so what with the grown-ups I reckon forty cornets will see it through.'

'Leave it to you,' I said.

'I'll be down soon after half past three.'

When they came, Fred could have been excused if he had been startled by their number. He had never seen so many children before, so many happy, shouting children, running up the path to the field, calling 'Happy birthday, Freddie!' This was a carnival of a party; a boy was dressed as the Mad Hatter, battered top hat and tails too big for him, another wore a huge mask of the March Hare, girls in party frocks with ribbons in their hair, boys chasing each other, all converging on Fred who stood his ground half-way up the slope of the field with ears pricked; and I would have forgiven him if he had turned and fled. Thirty-two children swarming towards him, screams of laughter, yells of glee, this cacophony of happiness made noise enough to scare him into leaping into the next field. He did not budge. He awaited the onslaught of arms being flung around him, ears pulled, mane ruffled, nose kissed and kissed again, pats on the back, tail tugged, as if it were an experience to which he had long been accustomed. All through the afternoon he allowed himself to be treated as a toy, and not once did he show impatience. Dear one-year-old Fred. This was indeed his hour of glory.

Penny, meanwhile, was having her own passage of fame. Fred, being too young to carry anyone, Penny had to play the role of the patient beach donkey. Can I have a ride? Can I? Can I? Up and down the field she went, solemnly and safely. Sometimes two astride her back, sometimes even three. She plodded on in the manner of a donkey who knew how to earn its living. She waited quietly as someone was heaved upon her back, she moved on at the right moment, she halted as soon as a fair ride had been completed. Can I have a ride? Can I? Can I?

There they were, two donkeys with ice-cream smeared about their faces, sucking lollipops; Fred a toy donkey, Penny a working one, when the time came for The Cake. Jeannie had made it, a table on the field was ready for it, and there was a single candle.

The air was still, and with ceremony the candle was lit. The table was at the bottom of the field above the wood and so its shelter helped the flame to burn steadily and with no fear of it flickering out. All around were Fred's guests. There was chattering and laughter, and from somewhere in the background a small voice began the customary birthday song.

'Too soon!' someone else shouted.

Fred, at that moment, had not arrived. He was a few yards away in a cluster of admirers, a girl with golden hair holding the halter, and all of them edging Fred towards the climax of his party. He did not want to be rushed. He was going to arrive in his own good time. And suddenly the shouts went up: 'Here's Freddie! Happy birthday, Freddie! Good old Freddie!' Treble voices sailing into the sky. A moment in time that many years away, most would remember. Nothing complicated. The same pleasure that centuries have enjoyed.

Fred reached the table. The candle on the cake, a strong, confident flame, awaited him. But I do not think anyone who was present believed he would so successfully fulfil their secret hopes.

As the children sang his birthday song, Fred pushed his head forward inquiringly towards the candle, snorted; and blew it out.

In this impermanent world in which restlessness is a deception for contentment, in which the individual can only salvage what he can from the twilight pressures of the mass, in which to be sensitive is no longer a grace, Jeannie and I could touch the old stones of Minack, brace ourselves before the gales, listen to the sea talking and to the gulls crying, be at one with the animals, have time to search our inward selves and fight the shadow which is the enemy; and to marvel at the magic which had led us to a life we loved so much.

The dying sun was beginning to touch the fields across the valley. The shadows of boulders were sharp. The pilchard fleet of Newlyn was busily setting out towards the Wolf Rock. A happy day. A soft breeze off the sea, curlews flying high and calling, a woodpecker laughing.

'Let's go and see the donkeys,' I said.

We reached the field and saw no sign of them.

'That's funny, I hope I didn't leave the gate open.'

'Look there they are!' said Jeannie.

At the far end of the field beneath the distant hedge I saw Penny standing dozily upright. On the grass beside her, lying outstretched, was Fred sound asleep. A donkey who had had a party, enjoyed every minute of it, and was now exhausted.

We did not disturb them.

Lama

The east wind blew on Christmas day, scything across the sea from the Lizard hidden in gloom. The black easterly. It slashed into our cliff, burning the meadows with the salt which came with it, tearing up the valley to the cottage, cutting into the cracks of window frames, rushing through the wood, screeching a message that bitter cold, cold weather was upon us. And when Lama asked to be let out, and I opened the door and she gaily stepped outside, she suddenly stopped when her whiskers met the wind. Good gracious no, she seemed to say to herself, much too cold; and immediately reversed into the cottage.

I heard Jeannie's mother call to me from the spare room: 'Merry Christmas!'

'*Merry Christmas!*' *I replied. '*Did you have a good sleep?*'*

Some enjoy the hallucination that if you tear up one part of your life and substitute another, congenial to your imagination, that you become immune to trouble. There is the gay, hopeful belief that if you can steel yourself to surrender the tedious, or tense, routine of life to which you have reluctantly become accustomed, problems inward and outward will dissolve. They do not. There is no such act as escapism. Wherever you go, whatever you do – emigrate, change jobs, find your dream cottage, pursue your true ambition – you have yourself as a companion; you have the same grim fight to earn a living. What you do gain, if you have the luck which Jeannie and I have had, is the chance to embrace the environment which you love, and which softens the blows when they come; for the expanse of sky helps to free us; so also the sense that the wild animals, the foxes, the badgers, have been going their mysterious ways for centuries; and the sea is as it always was. The reward, if you have the luck, is to become aware again that values have never changed, that true pleasure is as it has been since the beginning.

I had met people on occasions, those who possessed a special dottiness for cats, who claimed that as soon as a cat vacancy occurred it was broadcast cat fashion to all members of the local fraternity. Soon after Monty had died, for instance, I had met a sweet old lady in Penzance who said to me in a tone of irritating certainty, a charming, knowing smile pressing the point home: 'Don't you be upset about your Monty, Mr Tangye. Next on the list will soon be with you!'

'Rubbish,' I had replied, under my breath.

For the first time Jeannie's mother had brought Angus, her Scottie, with her. Angus had always been banned from Minack while Monty was alive, for Monty would never have allowed him into the cottage. He was a cheerful little dog; and because his home was a flat in London, Angus treated his walks around Minack as those in paradise. On this occasion Jeannie's mother returned from a walk, and as always when she was excited her trifle Scottish accent became delightfully pronounced.

'Did you know you have a little black cat on your land? Angus chased it, he did. Right through the daffodils at the top of the big field, and the wee thing disappeared over the hedge into the moor.'

My only reaction, an instinctive annoyance, was that such a chase should have been allowed to happen in the daffodil beds.

We were earning a living, we couldn't risk damage. Why wasn't Angus called off the chase?

But, as had happened once before when Monty came into my life, Jeannie's mother knew better. A damaged daffodil did not compare in value to a little black cat.

'Such a pretty wee thing it was,' she said; and looked at me.

'I've got cramp.'

'Turn over then.'

'I can't.'

'Why?'

'Lama's so comfortable.'

'Oh Heavens,' I said, 'so this game has started all over again.'

I don't mind admitting that I had greatly enjoyed the interval during which I had slept in comfort. Night hours and night hours during Monty's lifetime I had spent with limbs numbed while Monty lay against a leg or a foot, blissfully asleep at my expense. And now the performance was scheduled to start again.

'Don't you think,' I said gently, 'that it might be a good idea to have a new regime with Lama? After all she's been accustomed to sleep in any old place.'

'I can't wait to see *you* pushing her off the bed.'

Jeannie's knowledge of me was, of course, quite correct. The discomfort, the readiness for self-sacrifice, had always received its compensation when I stretched out my hand and touched a paw, or traced a finger on a forehead; for Monty all his life had provided me with reassurance during dismal wakes in early mornings, and now Lama could do the same. I was, therefore, defeating myself if I were so selfish as to try to ban her from a portion of the bed.

'Well,' I said, 'you're probably right.'

There was a pause.

'Lama,' murmured Jeannie, 'you've won.'

Cat lovers, I have found, those all-embracing lovers of

every kind of cat, show great irritation when their love receives little response. A battle of wills ensues and it sometimes appears to me that the cat lover, the alleged cat lover, is a bit heartless. Vanity is wounded when purrs do not immediately operate. Tempers are even frayed if the cat concerned remains obstinately aloof. Cats, it seems, are expected to throw their arms around their human lovers with the same enthusiasm as the latter throw their arms around cats. And if they don't the lover's knot is often cut. One day, for instance, after many people had visited us, Lama had gone to bed first and settled comfortably, as far as she was concerned, a few inches below my pillow. I tried, like a contortionist, to get in between the sheets without disturbing her; and while I was twisting my way past her, Lama watching me with a baleful eye, I suddenly caught sight of a gap in her fur, just at one side of her spinal column. I looked at it in astonishment. One of the visitors had cut away a tuft about an inch square.

I watched the Land-rover Jeannie driving, her mother beside her, splash through Monty's Leap, come up the last stretch of the lane past the stables, then round the steep piece to the right, and pull up in front of the window through which I was watching. The new coat, the new hat. I saw in the instant of watching that here again I was witnessing the wish to please. Not to be thought casual. An effort made, much thought before the choice was finally decided upon. Another Christmas, and yet seemingly no gap since the last one. Gaily wrapped parcels in the two suitcases in the well of the

Land-rover. Just the same as it always had been. Only the wink of an eyelid to note the passing of time.

I have never looked upon time as a hill, hiding the past on its side. Time to me is a plain, so that if the circumstances are right, if the associations are in union, the past can be seen like a fire; and the feelings repeated, recognised again after being forgotten, the old story of Citizen Kane remembering his beginning, of Marcel Proust's *madeleine*, of all our minds when we are not controlled by doctrine. You touch the past as if it were the present. You meet yourself again as a ten-year-old at a moment of anguish or great joy. You are there again at first love; nothing has changed, you are as you always have been.

Boris was heavy enough to make a sound on gravel like a person walking on the path. I have often heard the noise of his webbed feet and been deceived, and cried out to Jeannie: 'Somebody's coming!' But it was only Boris plodding up the path, wanting a piece of Jeannie's home-made bread, or just needing our company and feeling he would receive it by sentry-going on the soil and the plants of the small garden outside the door. But on this occasion he walked with stealth. A Muscovy drake's tip-toe. His beak had a target.

I arrived by chance at the greenhouse at the instant of strike. The supple softness of Lama was hopelessly vulnerable. There she lay, lost in her dreams, the careless abandon of a happy cat, a nymph at the mercy of the hypnotic powers of the sun; and I suddenly saw Boris a split second away from making his dab.

It is joyous to look at the meadows when the green sheaves of the daffodils are first bursting the soil. Bed upon bed of them, each brimming with hope for us who depend upon them for our livelihood. And part of the fun, sometimes the disappointment of the stroll is for me to bend down, and to pinch with my fingers the collar of the bulbs. Green leaves may be growing but this does not mean that flowers will follow; and you learn to feel whether or not a bud is on the way, and if you have pinched a number of them, spaced here and there in different beds, you come to know long before the daffodil harvest begins whether or not it is going to be successful. There are words of mine still floating on Minack cliffs. Contradictory words. Some belong to one season, some to another.

'Jeannie! There are no buds at all. None at all. It's going to be a terrible season.'

'Let's not be over confident . . . but I believe there are more buds this year than I've ever known before.'

'I'm nervous, Jeannie. There seem to be plenty of Obs, but the Mags seem terribly light.'

Jeannie and I have so many times looked at the meadows; and seen superimposed upon them our bank statement.

One can be tedious about Christmas. One can, in fact, be so tedious that it becomes a bore. In this enlightened

gimmick age, it is tedious to accept the idea that there can be one day in the year for which centuries demand goodwill; and so the excuse is made that it is too commercialised. That is true, of course. It is hopelessly commercialised. And yet this is still no reason to treat Christmas as an anachronism. For it will always be the time of old-fashioned kindness, of evidence of truth, of pure unselfishness and, quite often, of unexpected exultation. And so with these qualities as its armour, there is no cause for anyone to consider Christmas as a bore. It demands an effort. That's all.

In the afternoon, the day before Christmas Eve, Lama arranged herself on my lap. Up to that moment I had been busy. I had promised Jeannie, for instance, to clear my desk and there were other tasks on my schedule. Then Lama jumped up after I, in a moment of laziness, had sat down on the sofa to glance at the paper; only for a second to glance at the headlines, no intention of

avoiding my responsibilities. But there on my knees was
Lama.

She began to purr. It was not one of those ordinary
purrs which one must admit are two a penny in any
normal cat-happy circumstances. It was a roar. A glorious anthem praising to the heavens that she was the
favoured one to live alone with us inside the cottage at
Minack. It was a great burst of Christmas wishes. An
expression of innocent delight that the three of us were
together. And as I listened to her, drawing a finger up
and down her black silky back, guilty about the things
I should be doing but hypnotically relaxed by the sound
of her, I heard a car draw up outside; then footsteps
coming to the door.

It is always a challenge if duty demands that you
should remove a contented cat from your lap. Insensitive people throw them to the floor without more ado.
Others pray it will make its decision on its own. I heard
the knock, thankfully saw Lama leap away from me,
got up and went to open the door. A telegram!

'May I spend Christmas with you unless family gathering. Jack.'

I hadn't seen him in years. I thought he was in
America.

Jackie Broadbent was a legendary figure in the world
of newspaper men.

The east wind blew on Christmas day, scything across
the sea from the Lizard hidden in gloom. The black
easterly. It slashed into our cliff, burning the meadows
with the salt which came with it, tearing up the valley

to the cottage, cutting into the cracks of window frames, rushing through the wood, screeching a message that bitter cold, cold weather was upon us. And when Lama asked to be let out, and I opened the door and she gaily stepped outside, she suddenly stopped when her whiskers met the wind. Good gracious, no, she seemed to say to herself, much too cold; and immediately reversed into the cottage.

I heard Jeannie's mother call to me from the spare room: 'Merry Christmas!'

'Merry Christmas!' I replied. 'Did you have a good sleep?'

It was my job to take Jackie Broadbent his morning tea; he was in the bunching shed on a camp bed. He had arrived in the late afternoon of Christmas Eve; and with him he had brought a leather valise like a cricket bag in which were his clothes for the stay, and several half bottles of champagne.

There was a frost in the wind and I took Jackie his tea in a thermos Jeannie had filled. I unscrewed the top and poured out the tea. 'Merry Christmas!' I said. Then added, laughing, 'So you were wide awake all the time I was looking after your welfare lighting the stoves.'

'Wide awake? I've been wide awake all night. What else do you expect a man to do lying on a bed belonging to World War One, reminding him of the idiocy of the human race?'

'Sorry it was so uncomfortable.'

'Forty-five years ago men slept on this bed dreaming of the greatness of the British Empire, girls, drink, white supremacy, the glory of dying for a brave new world, contentment, riches, all the delusions that lead men to their end.'

'You are cheerful.'

'I'm so cheerful I could dance.' And he kicked his legs up and down under the bedclothes. I feared the camp bed might collapse.

'Anyhow it's Christmas.'

'Don't be so sentimental. Three quarters of the world have never heard of Christmas.'

'Listen,' he said, 'as I lay shivering in this bed I heard the guns of Passchendaele. The primitive guns which could only kill a dozen at a time, perhaps two, perhaps more, it doesn't matter. And I saw the leaders of opinion, the usual lot . . . the politicians hiding behind generals, the churchmen, the societies which are manipulated by local ambitious men and women. I saw them not only in this country but in all countries. There they were, all desperately earnest in their fashion, intoxicated by a flag and a symbol, simple people elevated by luck to leadership of the rabble. All of them both sides, were sincere in committing their faults or virtues. But . . .' and he now realised his pipe had gone out and stopped talking to light it again '. . . but . . . that generation which slept on beds like this one were only toying with war.'

'Obviously,' I said calmly, 'despite the losses.'

'Yes, yes, I know the point you're making . . . but don't you see that the minds of men and women haven't kept pace with the machines of war?'

'I do,' I said, 'but minds never have done.'

'Ah,' he said, 'you're thinking I'm talking about the

Great Powers. I am not. They have their own histories to guide them and steer them clear of trouble unless there is an accident. Mark my words . . . Russia will come to terms with America before long. They're safe. It's the juvenile government I'm thinking of. No history to them, no Passchendaele to tell them of war. An atom bomb is a plaything in their primitive political struggles, a trivial ally to their shouts. Sooner or later the bomb will be the revolutionary weapon. It will not be the deterrent. That's what I was thinking about on this Passchendaele bed.'

It was time to shut up Boris, and this time I opened the door and went with Lama, then down the path across the grass by the greenhouse and into the wood. There in the old chicken house, the size of a palace as far as Boris is concerned, room for thirty Muscovy drakes not one, sat Boris on his perch craning his neck forwards and gently hissing. 'Goodnight, Boris,' I said, and locked the door. He was such an imperious character that one felt in dutybound to say the words, 'good night'; and sometimes when I had absent-mindedly forgotten to do so, I used foolishly to return and shout the words through the door. As if it were a talisman of good luck to wish him goodnight.

I paused every few yards waiting for Lama to catch up with me, and when I reached the onion meadow I sat down on a low stone hedge; and a minute later she had jumped up on my knees, settling herself like a glossy

black cushion, and
began gently to purr.
It was a heavenly day,
a day when the sea
was a cornflower
blue; and fringing the
arm of the Lizard
across the Bay was a
billowy line of white
clouds. The sun shone
on the long stretch of
sands at Looe Bar, and

below me a few hundred yards offshore there were a half
dozen small boats grouped together, with tiny figures
leaning over their sides feathering a shoal of mackerel.
It was very still, an Indian summer day; and to my left
was Carn Barges, a huge rock balanced upright as if it
were a sentinel. Beyond was Carn Dhu which juts out
from the far side of Lamorna Cove, sheltering the Cove
with high, grey boulder-strewn cliffs, this lovely cove
which on a day like this has the stillness of a South
Sea lagoon; and forever reminds me of Cook's Bay in
Moorea. I sat there listening to the curlews calling as
they swept across the sky high above me, to a robin
singing a sad song, to the sudden laugh of a green
woodpecker which see-sawed its way inland to my
right, to the throb of a French crabber with emerald
green hull heading for Newlyn, to the sea touching the
rocks like the swish of a gentle wind through trees; and
to Lama purring.

This was one of those naive moments when one
would like to tear away from their anchors the sad and

the tired and the bored; to refresh and awaken them by
the feel of a Cornish day when the sea is a cornflower
blue. Here is a gift which has no need of man's interference. Here is permanence, the unbending bridge
between the past and the present which gives the human
soul its base. Brains are no asset at such moments. All
that is required is an attitude of mind which is capable
of exultation, a heart that soars as it watches; a human
being who has purged himself of aiming to conquer by
logic. No brittle questions need be asked. No detached
observance. Just the ability to catch the fleeting awareness that there can be moods which do not belong to
reason. Another dimension enters your life amid the
solitude and the grandeur; and suddenly there is a
stranger within yourself.

The only entrance to our cliff was through this gate at
the top. It was no place for strangers. There was a deep
cleft biting into the land, a sheer fall to the sea below,
guarding one boundary of the meadows; and the other
boundary disappeared into boulders, brambles, gorse
and, in summer, a forest of bracken. Below were the
rocks, granite and blue elvan pitted with fissures, huge
ungainly shapes, each part of the whole which sloped
without plan inevitably to the sea. Here the seaweed,
draped like an apron, thickened the water at low tide;
and gulls, oystercatchers, and turnstones poked among
it, uttering wild cries. There was the sense of loneliness,
and yet of greatness. This was unmanageable nature, the
freedom man chases.

And to us the cliff reflected our endeavour since we

came to Minack. It was part of ourselves. We had seen it those years ago when it was untamed, and visioned the meadows we would carve from the undergrowth, the rich crops we would grown, the sure future we would build. Here we had been a part of some victories and many defeats. We had seen harvests of early potatoes lashed by a gale and destroyed in a night. We had laboured on hot summer days on this cliff shovelling with a long-handled Cornish spade beneath the potato plants. Jeannie on hands and knees picking up potatoes and filling the sacks, then the long steep climb to the top, a sack at a time, journey after journey.

We had rejoiced in the flower season at the sight of the daffodils, dazzling yellow against the blue sea, gulls high above, gannets plummeting offshore; then gladly endured the steady task of picking, gathering an armful and slowly filling a basket; and the climb again, heavy basket in either hand. Such as this was our victory. Here in remoteness, a sense of communication with the base of beauty. Not victory in a worldly sense. We produced. We were two of the losing originals. When our efforts left our environment, so did our control. Far away people, cool in their calculations, undisturbed by our hopes, beset with their own problems, decreed our reward.

We had our shield. Moments like the quiet of a Christmas morning when Jeannie and I were together, with a cat called Lama who was born within the sound of the sea.

The Way to Minack

Most of the important decisions of my life had been taken in London and each decision had ended a phase which I thought at the time was permanent. Of course the stress behind a decision is easily forgotten when you are far away from its environment; and yet each decision has built another part of you, sharing the responsibility of whatever happens.

I marvel at those who neatly analyse themselves and the rest of us. The motion of living appears so simple after reading the views of the theory boys on this or that. Summaries of their solutions possess no edge of doubt. A huge house of cards is made to look indestructible. There is no grey in any problem. Reason is king. And although I distrust such exponents of logic, there goes with my mood a certain admiration. I admire their confidence because facts, in my own experience, so often lie, mocking the conclusions based upon them. I am, therefore, unable to pigeon-hole myself. I am a don't know. I wend a long way round to find a solution to any problem, and when in the end I come to a decision it is usually instinct that motivates it. An inner force which I do not understand pushes me into action, so that afterwards I have to try and make the facts fit the deed. This, I know, is untidy behaviour and it sometimes lets me down. I find myself saying things, for instance, which do not do me justice. I blurt out a sentence which self-discipline would have made me smother, and I declare something which the listener interprets as the truth.

It is the woman who makes the sacrifice. It is easy for a man to exchange comfort for the primitive, to brace himself to accept a new way of living, to switch environment; but for Jeannie it meant giving up a suite of offices at the Savoy, entertaining the famous in her role as a public relations officer, and becoming instead a housewife in a cottage without running water or electricity. This was ambition in reverse. This was the kind of action which the conventional expect to see fail. Our acquaintances waited expectantly. How long will she last in Cornwall? And over the years Jeannie has been monotonously asked by kinder-minded people:

'Wouldn't you like to go back to the life you used to lead in London?'

I have found myself at dull parties making a sensational remark or asking a pertinent question just in order to stir the pool of dullness. My attitude seldom succeeds in its object because the conventionality that breeds dullness retreats from challenge. I make a remark to awake the commonplace, and the response to it is often so dampening that I too feel dull. I am, therefore, on guard when someone tries to awaken my own lassitude; and I was aware that this was what George Brown was trying to do. In such a situation I am anxious, over-anxious, to be as bright as my companion would like me to be; but in my mood, if my temperament at the moment is engulfed by mental cotton wool, I am inclined to conduct myself like an inexperienced school-boy. I flounder. I react with a foolishness so that hours, weeks, months, sometimes a year later, I remember the moment with shame. A self-inflicted wound which no one else has observed.

I received one day an invitation to an elegant literary party in London.

I had once before been invited to a literary party, and the occasion has haunted me ever since. It was a month before war broke out and I had just spent a year travelling the world, and I was writing a travel book. On the way to the lunch the chairman of the occasion asked me to make a speech, and he said that all he required were anecdotes of my journey which would make the listeners laugh. I sat nervously through the soup, roast lamb, pêche melba and coffee, until the chairman rose to his feet.

'John Gielgud,' he said to the expectant few hundred, 'was to speak today but is unable to do so. J. B. Priestley was to take his place but he suddenly had to go abroad. I was then lucky enough to persuade John Steinbeck but three days ago he went down with flu . . . and so we have Derek Tangye.'

The faint applause which greeted this introduction still whispers in my memory. So too does the quiet murmur which followed my anecdotal speech.

If you live with someone and there are no office hours to separate you, no other life to lead, one has to be on guard against the groove. There you are, fulfilling the halcyon dream, two people who have come together, the end achieved which you hoped for at the beginning, daylight hours shared, boss to each other; and yet unless you remain separate, each a subtle stranger to the other, dullness sets in. There must be no quenching of conflict. Each sometimes must be misunderstood. Propinquity must be allowed victory because conventional happiness has been won.

Most of the important decisions of my life had been taken in London and each decision had ended a phase which I thought at the time was permanent. Of course the stress behind a decision is easily forgotten when you are far away from its environment; and yet each decision has built another part of you, sharing the responsibility of whatever happens.

I knew, therefore, what I had to do, I would set out to remember the kind of life I used to lead. I would go to see the places in London where I lived, and seek to catch my mood at the time when the decisions were being made. First, 38 Cranley Gardens off the Old Brompton Road, where I arrived as an innocent from Harrow to become an office boy in Unilever House; then Joubert Studios off the King's Road where I spent an idle summer; then 20 Elm Park Lane, also in Chelsea; then I would remember 56 Portsmouth Street, Manchester; then Cholmondeley House where I was to carry Jeannie across the threshold after our marriage; then Thames Bank Cottage at Mortlake where ghosts, I feel sure, will always shout on Boat Race day. All these in their different fashion led the way to Minack.

A westerly gale was blowing the night we left Minack; and the roar was as if the cottage were a boat, the roof and walls the rigging. Outside, as I carried the suitcases down the path to the car which was taking us to Penzance station, I was pushed so violently by the wind that I had to drop the suitcases and steady myself. Far away across the bay, the Lizard light winked. The darkness hid the outline of the land around me but there in the distance curving towards the Lizard were the lights of Prah sands, Porthleven and Mullion. No sign of what was in between, only the sound of the sea's rage.

There is something opulent about the leather smell of a taxi, and now we were speeding through Bayswater and on into Park Lane, I felt the excitement of our adventure. An early morning in London, no traffic, no one yet to crowd the pavements, Jeannie at my side, familiar sights to please, the Vickers building and the Hilton to shock. I was nervous but happy. I was, for instance, about to wear the cloak of a millionaire. Money was about to lose its control of me. Along Constitution Hill and into the Mall, then round Trafalgar Square and into the Strand. In a minute we would be turning into the Savoy courtyard. In a minute bank notes would take the place of pennies. I had my arm through Jeannie's and I pressed her hand.

We went through the revolving glass doors into the foyer, the familiar pillars, the sofas and chairs to the left where people sit to watch the world go by, the stairs past the Grill leading up to the American Bar. And on the right the flower kiosk, the bookstall where Jeannie had arranged for *Time Was Mine* to be displayed, the counter of the Enquiry Office, and a little further along, that of Reception with suave young men in morning coats already on duty. Ahead were the stairs leading down to the Restaurant and to the corridor off which were the private banqueting rooms and the lift which took guests to that side of the building; and ahead, too, were the stairs and the passage which score upon score of times Jeannie had walked as she went to and from Room 205 which was her office. There, too, were the news tape machines which men pretend to look at while waiting hopefully for an expected companion, and the lift which Bert, the liftman, had never left while the bombs fell, and the alcove of telephone boxes where Abel had ruled in an orderly confusion of telephone calls.

'Miss Nicol!'

The welcome had started. A hall porter in his dove-grey uniform came forward. Then another. And this was to continue during the first days, as staff came on to their different rosters. The clerks of the Enquiry office, the waiters of Grill and Restaurant, those of the American Bar, other people who worked behind the scenes . . . another and another would come up to her remembering.

We were on the fifth floor, and the young man turned to his right, and we went along the corridor, and when we reached the end, the key opened the door of a river suite. 'We stood at the window of our suite on the fifth floor of the Savoy Hotel,' wrote Charles Chaplin in his autobiography on the occasion he came back to live in Europe with his wife Oona. 'We stood silent, drinking in the most stirring view of a city in all this world.'

When we were left alone, we too stood at the window. It was huge, like a shop's window, and it was divided into three sections and one section was ajar, so that as we stood there we heard the waking hum of London. Away to our right were the Houses of Parliament with the face of Big Ben clearly to be seen; and across the curve of the river were Hungerford and Westminster bridges. Opposite, and incongruous because it seemed to emerge from a patchwork of haphazard buildings, was the Festival Hall; and to the right of it were the eyesockets of the Shell monolith. Sleek tugs and their barges were busy on the river as the tide was high, and we were reminded again how long it had been since we had lived in London; for the tugs we knew when we had our cottage at Mortlake were as T-Model Fords to the cars of today. Below us Cleopatra's Needle peered above the bare plane trees of the Embankment Gardens, and I thought of its curious connection with my family . . . it was hoisted into place by hydraulic jacks invented by my grandfather and his brothers, and one jack lies in the foundation to this day. On the left was Waterloo Bridge, and black beetles were beginning to scurry across it to their shops and offices; and Jeannie remembered how she was once one of them on her way to Room 205. Further to the left, past the spick and span *Discovery*, I could see Blackfriars and the Unilever building into which I once scurried myself. And if it had been clear, if there had been no clinging early morning haze, we would have seen ahead of us the hills, the surprising hills of Wandsworth, Lambeth and Lewisham; and beyond them those of Surrey.

'A good beginning,' I said.

'Marvellous,' said Jeannie laughing. And she picked up a telephone and ordered breakfast.

There was an oak door at 38 Cranley Gardens. I used to face it late at night when I had forgotten my key, staring at its threatening solidity, wondering whether I could dare ring the bell and, after a jittery interval, have the courage to face my landlady in her dressing gown.

'If you forget your key once more, Mr Tangye . . .'

I left my two comfortable top-floor rooms at 38 Cranley Gardens on my twenty-second birthday, and went to live at Joubert Studios in Jubilee Place off the King's Road, Chelsea.

My single room faced an alleyway and saw no sun, a lugubrious place; but to me it seemed like a palace because it was another step towards my emancipation. My aim in life at this time was to rid myself of the strait-jacket standards my environment had brought me up to believe indestructible, and to find a way to be free of the restlessness inside me. I had no clue where this restlessness might lead me but, if I bottled it up, I knew I would never find happiness; and so leaving Cranley Gardens meant leaving conformism, and moving to Chelsea meant moving to intangible freedom.

'All I want out of life,' I wrote in my diary that first evening at Joubert Studios, 'is to be able to say at the end of it that I have lived vividly.'

One morning I received a pound note from my father and with it came a message: 'Keep your pecker up. It's going to be all right soon.' And so it was. That lunch time I called in at the Six Bells in the King's Road. Some people I knew were there, and one of them introduced me to a pretty girl; and while I spent my pound note I learnt from her that she had a boyfriend who was closely acquainted with Max Aitken son of Lord Beaverbrook. By closing time she had promised to introduce me to her boyfriend. Within a fortnight I had been ushered into Max Aitken's office in the *Daily Express* building in Fleet Street. Within another fortnight I was in Manchester.

I had been given a month's trial as a *Daily Express* reporter.

I was away from London for eighteen months; and when I came back I wore a brown trilby hat jauntily aslant to my eyes, and I dangled a cigarette out of the corner of my mouth. I had begun my trial period in Manchester as an assistant to the night news reporter, roaming round Manchester until half past four in the morning, calling at hospitals and police stations, keeping in touch with fire brigades, seeking news of casualties and crime and fires. On my second night I was in Ancoats Hospital when an ambulance brought in a man who had just been found dead in the street; nothing unusual about that, just one of several incidents during the year. The dour, kind, blunt Yorkshireman, the chief night news reporter, offered me a chance to write up the facts. My first story. A man found dead in the street . . . but could I write it? The permutations of such a story were innumerable, and I tried them all. Five lines were required, yet I found it impossible to discover the magic formula; until at last . . .

> Charles Kemp, aged eighty-five, of Garden Street, Ardwick, Manchester, collapsed in the street late last night, and on being taken to Ancoats Hospital was found to be dead.

I was launched as a reporter.

I became alive in Manchester; and I loved the wet dreary streets and the rattle of trams, the good fellowship in rumbustious pubs and the gaiety of my colleagues; and the excitement of being part of a far wider world than I had ever known before. I began to learn to judge people for what they were worth and not for what they appeared to be; and my role of reporter, however harsh and trivial the missions could sometimes be, had begun to teach me that all men are not equal; and, like racehorses, they cannot all win.

I was always happy in Manchester, and I realised that I would never again enjoy the same undergraduate spirit of freedom. Yet I could not smother the urge to go forward. Manchester had awakened my senses, but London was where I belonged.

I stayed at first with my father and mother who had rented a furnished house for a few weeks in Elm Park Gardens in Chelsea, a high storey house of endless stairs; and I used to hurry back to them from my unsettled kind of day, and climb the stairs to my room, and say to myself that although I loved my parents their normality did not fit with my unreliability, and I wished I was on my own. I did not have to tell my mother this in words and, without saying anything to me, she began to look for a flat for me. And one evening, after I had arrived home late for dinner, irritable because I had left friends enjoying themselves, she broke the news that she had found for me the ideal flat.

It was not a flat. It was a mews cottage . . . and it was ideal. If was off Elm Park Road, between The Vale and

Beaufort Gardens, both leading to the King's Road, and the address was 20 Elm Park Garden Mews; you came to it after passing under a brick archway which seemed to have no reason for being there. It was a little street which ran towards the Fulham Road, and at the beginning of my living there it was a working street with chauffeurs coming and going in limousines; and these were always being washed and polished and tinkered with while children played noisily around watching their fathers in overalls, and watching them again in peaked caps and dark uniforms as they drove from the mews on the way to their dignified assignments. Then as people like myself moved in, and others who remodelled the cottages in fancy ways, the mood of the mews changed and the chauffeurs who remained became the odd men out; and there came a day when the authorities no longer considered it a mews and they changed the name to Elm Park Lane.

The front door of the mews cottage opened up on a tiny stairway and this led straight up into the sitting-room which had a wooden balustrade, like that of a minstrel's gallery, overlooking the stairway. There was a bedroom, a kitchen, a bathroom like a box room because it had no windows. Beneath the sitting-room was a garage, and on the left of the front door was a ground floor spare room, which was to be used by my brother Nigel when he came to London on visits from where he lived in Hertfordshire. The place was unfurnished and dilapidated but my mother, while I worked, supervised the decorating and went bargain hunting for furniture. I still have some of the furniture; the sofa is at Minack, and the kitchen cupboard which came from

Peter Jones is in the barn behind a pile of fertiliser bags; and its contents are now nuts and bolts, and half used tins of paint. So the day came when I moved into the first home of my own; I realised it was another of the original pleasures, and I felt I could conquer the world.

I realised now that the time had come for me to leave 20 Elm Park Lane, and that when I did so I would in effect be saying goodbye to my youth. There I lived the gay days when there were oceans of time in which to make mistakes and to recover from them; and to be in despair at one moment but be filled with hope the next because there were so many years ahead. I lived there the time which one never expects to end, the ebullience of being young and successful, of passing fancies, of dominating views, of believing all youth is Peter Pan.

In the New Year I had begun to spend two nights a week at the Savoy, and my book *Time Was Mine* was published, and I met Jeannie; after the second occasion of having dinner with her, a bomb hit the hotel killing two guests. The Savoy was the headquarters of the American journalists, indeed of all top journalists, and it was useful for me to be with them. They all hovered round Jeannie who was barely out of her teens, and who was just beginning her reign as the most famous public relations officer the Savoy has ever had. She introduced them to the people they want to meet, booked their rooms, flirted with them, and was all the while in gentle fashion seeing they were happy in London; and in so doing she was able often to influence their reports on Britain.

'Will you marry me?' It was seven o'clock in the Coalhole, the pub in the Strand, and I had been waiting for her for an hour; and she had expected a row as she came up to the marble-topped table where I was sitting.

'Yes,' she said quickly, glad to be let off.

We were married in the Lady's Chapel of Richmond Parish Church at a quarter past twelve on 20 February, and the reception was held at Cholmondeley House overlooking the Thames down Friars Lane, where I now lived.

We had presented ourselves to the Vicar three weeks beforehand, and after agreeing to marry us he asked me to pay his fee. I pulled out my cheque book and started to write. 'I don't accept cheques,' the Vicar said smartly. And as I had no cash, Jeannie had to look in her purse and produce the money; and she says I never paid her back.

'I was in Harvey Nichols this morning' said Jeannie calmly as she was cooking my dinner, Monty looking at her hopefully, 'when the warning buzzers went and we all lay flat among the rolls of carpet on the ground floor. We heard a V1 pass overhead, and then we all got up. A moment later we heard another coming, and we all fell on the floor again.'

I would ring up Jeannie from my office when I heard a crash in the Savoy direction and saw a plume of smoke.

All right? 'Yes, it was in Kingsway.' Or she would ring me. And a slang developed among people. 'OK it's gone over' ... 'OK I heard it drop' ... 'This is a near one, get down' ... 'Poor devils, I should think it's Sloane Street'. And there were the clouds, the endless low clouds that summer which let the V1's fly unseen, and the questions which were asked: 'On which side is God?' Thus did people live and think and fear, and have a purpose.

I always found it difficult to get down to facts with my MI5 colleagues. There was so much secrecy within secrecy. My colleagues were charming and amiable, conscientious and erudite, but sometimes when I was talking to one of them a glazed expression would come over his face; and I would try to make up my mind whether he was hiding information from me or whether he felt at a disadvantage because I had shown I knew more than he did. And on occasions I felt like a small boy unwillingly let into a prefects' pow wow ... for a sudden change of subject would take place just as I was beginning to be interested.

Jeannie loved her job. She was, however, a wise person. She had as much fun as anyone could wish for, but the pleasure from it was tempered slowly but surely by the realisation that the same kind of fun was being endlessly repeated; and that one day she would weary of it. Moreover in wartime there was a purpose for her work, worthwhile achievements were to be gained by her efforts; but in peacetime she was often made use of by those with trivial intentions. Some would try to lure her co-operation in a publicity stunt, others would earnestly ask her help, only to forget her once she had given it. She gradually became distrustful of people; and yet, and this was the charm of her, she was always ready to trust again.

We had a happy time in London. There was no doubt about that. Holiday London was a wonderful place. Yet we could not separate ourselves from the past. The past came bouncing into the present as we met again the same pressures which had led us to leave all those years ago.

There were the same languid bus queues, the same barging when the bus arrived; the same surge of people streaming across the Strand out of Charing Cross station in the morning, then nine hours later streaming back. There was the same unbearably stuffy heat in the big stores with sales staff despairingly counting the hours; the same blocks of grey, expressionless faces on tube platforms waiting for trains which were already full. All these were as we remembered them. But now there was also the screeching noise in the sky to add to that on the ground, and the sinister stalking of traffic wardens, and danger at night. 'I was attacked in the Embankment Gardens the other night,' one old member of the Savoy staff told us.

Spring had come to Minack while we were away.

'It has been very warm,' Geoffrey said when he met us off the train at Penzance, 'and the daffs have come in with a flood. The flower house is full of them.'

There was a pleasant reassurance in his words. I was sleepy and tired and a little dazed, and I was glad to be shocked into reality.

'Mostly Mags from the cliffs,' Geoffrey went on, 'they've jumped. And I picked eight baskets of Golden Harvest from the wood yesterday.'

He continued to talk about the daffodils as we drove beside the sea towards Newlyn, then up steep Paul Hill, then along the winding road towards Minack.

'What about the donkeys and Lama and Boris?'

'Good as gold.'

'Didn't they miss us?' Jeannie asked hopefully.

'Didn't notice you'd gone,' he answered, smiling.

We changed and had a quick breakfast, and then went down to the flower house. Rows of galvanised pails stood on the benches, each pail jammed with daffodils in bud. In the old days we would have had to force them into full bloom before they were ready to send away, but now the public is wiser. There is value for money when buds are bought.

'Heavens, Geoffrey,' I said, 'there are a lot here.'

'Sixty dozen I reckon.' He was already bunching. 'Not much time to waste,' he added firmly, 'if we're to catch the flower train.'

A Cornish Summer

*Most of us conform. We stifle the secret hopes we have
for personal freedom but find we cannot kill them. They
were with us before we were smoothed by habit; and
though sometimes they seem to fade away as the years
pass, we suddenly find ourselves faced with them again
in the form of frustration. There they are, challenging
our weak selves, demanding why we have betrayed
them.*

Expediency, we reply, we had to earn a living.

When did it happen? Three, five, ten summers ago?
Incidents merge into each other leaving timeless inter-

vals. I do not remember the summer when the drought dried up Monty's Leap, or the summer when I killed an adder outside our door, or the summer when a hoopoe paraded on the grass in front of the cottage, or the summer when I caught a conger eel in my lobster pot, and scared Jeannie when I brought it to her in the kitchen. Important incidents at the time, they have faded into one summer; so too have the pleasant hours I have watched Lama, the little black cat, and Boris, the Muscovy drake, sitting incongruously side by side, the one purring, the other ready to raise his head feathers and hiss harmlessly the second he was disturbed. So too have faded in memory the stares of Penny and Fred the donkeys, looking down at us from the field above our porch, demanding our attention.

When did it happen? I do not know which summer it was when we watched the fox cubs playing in the field on the other side of the shallow valley, fearing that some stranger would see them too, and disturb them. All soft-scented days when woodpigeons clapped their wings in courtship, when a raven grunted overhead, when green woodpeckers called to each other in the wood, belong to one summer; all still nights when the voices of fishermen, a mile or more out to sea sounded so loud that they were like ghosts talking in the front garden. There are no dates in my memory. No dates until this summer.

High above are the meadows we used to rent, years ago, for the growing of early potatoes. It was a period when we believed that an eldorado lay in the production of new potatoes. We grew them already on our own land, but we were greedy, and we imagined ourselves becoming the largest growers of new potatoes in West Cornwall, and so we rented these meadows. We loved them in the beginning, then grew to fear them. The ground was stony and in dry springs the potato plants refused to grow; and in wet springs when the plants were lush, a gale would come and scythe them, blackening the leaves so that only the useless stalks were left. We slaved in these meadows yet, because of this hard labour, a remnant of affection remains in our memories of the time we spent there. I walked around them the other day, and I found an old boot still lying in one of the hedges . . . a boot which had to be cut from my foot after my rotovator had overturned and one of the tines had pierced my foot. The ancient construction of galvanised iron known as the pink hut, partly hidden by laurel is still there . . . the pink hut where we used to sprout our potato seed, and where we once helped to nurse a badger back to health after it had been caught in a gin trap. And still I can see in my mind those who aided us in our work. St Just miners who came between shifts to pick up the potatoes; Geoffrey Semmens, fast shoveller from St Buryan who had to leave after one disastrous potato harvest but who for long has been back with us; and Jane, and Shelagh. I can see a picture of Jane on a blazing May afternoon, barefooted, fair hair falling over her shoulders, pausing from her task of scratching in the ground for potatoes, and picking up a long-handled shovel, then waving it angrily at an aircraft overhead because, it was rumoured, it had a device which detected uranium . . . Jane who came to us when she was just fifteen, lived in a cottage edging the cliff near by and hated progress. And I can see Shelagh, a year older than Jane, wistful, tragic little waif who would suddenly break the silence as we filled the potato baskets: 'Do you know there are only one hundred and ninety-six shopping days to Christmas?' We would laugh.

I had seen the first swallows of the year the day the daffodil harvest was over. I was standing late in the afternoon a few yards away from the cottage on what is called the bridge. The spot has no resemblance to a bridge, and it only received its name because, when standing or sitting there, you have a panoramic view before you . . . as if you were on the bridge of a ship. On summer days we spent much idle time on the bridge. We have levelled part of an old stone wall with dark blue slate at table height, and we sit on a bench in front of it. The wall is a wide one, and there is enough room for a narrow strip of earth above the dark blue slate; and this is encased in stone so that we have a flower bed as well on the wall. We grow mignonette there every summer, and on still days and evenings the air is full of its sweet scent.

When the swallows arrive, and the whitethroats, and the chiff-chaffs and the warblers, and other migratory birds, the holiday season has begun. Robins, wrens, blue tits and coal tits, hedge sparrows and dunnocks and all the other birds who never move a mile or two from their base, find the foreigners pecking about beside them. Favourite perches at night are occupied; and nesting sites. And a branch which a robin thought was his own is now the branch whence a flycatcher from Morocco dashes on his short-lived expeditions. This is the beginning of a period of justifiable upset among the local inhabitants. Cornwall is under occupation in woods, gardens, shore and towns. But the donkeys, within the restriction of their own standards, are at peace. Holiday-makers will be coming to flatter them. Cameras will be pointing at them. Rides will be asked for by shy children. The summer is their time.

We watched the first swallow soar and swoop over the wood for a minute or two, then on it flew towards Lamorna valley. Others would be following but the first, it is always the first, that one remembers. It meant the prospect of summer, and the coming of unexpected adventures, and the gentle illusion that we were as young as we always had been. We stood silently on the bridge. This was one of its pleasures that we could sit or stand there, gazing our lives away. There were so many small incidents taking place that were of great importance to ourselves, but would not appear important to those who have to drive themselves to pursue conventional values. Why waste time observing a fox, the same fox you saw yesterday and the day before, nosing about looking for mice? Why be surprised again at the way the rabbits sit on their hind legs like a dog doing a begging trick, watching the fox at a distance? Why not bolt for a hole? Why does the fox if he is looking for food pass them by, except for token attacks? What was that wild cry? A water rail? There is a green woodpecker rapping at the trunk of an elm tree in the wood. Which one? And are the blue tits nesting in the box we nailed to the tree by the camellia? The willow tree is greening. I'm glad the flowers of the cherry tree have not been spoilt by a gale this year. The *Scillonian* is late, isn't she? She's coming round the point now. The Stephenson's fishing fleet went out this morning so the weather will be staying fine. What glorious colours the French paint their crabbers . . . look at the brilliant green of that one. I saw her last week in Newlyn harbour. Someone is coming down the lane. No, false alarm.

It is not an easy age for peace of mind. The dull and unimaginative can achieve a version of it, as too those young enough who still believe that youth is everlasting, so too can those who are ruthlessly ambitious, so too the men and women who are so busy organising other people's lives that they forget to organise their own. All these have peace of mind of a kind. They do not suffer the pain of self questioning and remorse. They are certain that their standards are the right standards. They are normal.

But the rest of us, those of us who have to endure the doubts and personal complexities imposed by our imaginations, are labelled maladjusted and insecure, inferior beings in fact. It is curious how the phrase that he or she is 'insecure' has become a phrase that means a bad mark. As for myself, I do not understand how any human being can feel secure in the modern sense of the word unless he is unbearably conceited. Philosophy, after all, is based on the premise that those who are trying to find the truth about themselves have a sense of insecurity. Aristotle, Tagore, de Keyserling, any philosopher throughout the ages indeed, would have had no place in history if present values existed in their time. Contemplation was the motive power of their faith, periods of loneliness developed the truth of their wisdom. I wonder in what category an appointments bureau would place them if they were living today. Is there any doubt that they would be considered maladjusted and insecure?

One therefore has to try and find out about oneself against the wishes of convention. Convention needs to pump knowledge into you, not wisdom. Convention, in order to preserve what it represents, must act in the manner of a dictatorship, forcing each person to follow patterns of behaviour which, however distasteful to him, however ugly, result in the end with the declaration: 'I've got used to it.' The most repeated, the most despairing phrase of this period of the twentieth century.

When disgruntled people in the cities march to meetings on May Day holding high their banners of protest, the white flowers of the blackthorn lie in drifts in Minack woods and along the shallow valley which slopes towards the sea.

Chunky patches of golden gorse line the lane to the farm at the top of the hill, blue periwinkle spatters the banks; late primroses, wild violets, and early pink campion shelter amidst the growing grass. Fields of our neighbours where they have sown spring corn are covered by a film of green: white blossom clusters on the pear tree which we planted two years ago; and by the wooden plank which crosses Monty's Leap, the sticky leaves of the *Trachycarpus* exude their exotic scent.

'Persian Carpet' wallflowers colour the beds around the cottage. Aubrieta, white and mauve, falls over moss-covered stones. Dandelions are beginning to prove their invincibility again, piercing the joints of the stones in the path outside the cottage door. Foolish bumble bees buzz against the glass of the porch. A cuckoo, dip-ping its tail, calls on the rock at Carn Barges. A vixen in the lane in the afternoon warns us that cubs have made her fearless. A wren sings among the willows beside the stream. The first bluebells are in flower down the cliff. A blackbird in the elderberry close to the barn proclaims that she has a nest nearby. Rabbits chase each other in the field opposite. Last year's tadpoles crawl as

frogs from hibernating hideouts. The sunset is notice-
ably further to the west. Woodpigeons hurry to and
from the wood; larks sing above the field behind the
bridge; small birds perform aerobatics in their
excitement; gulls' cries have an enlarged vocabulary.
This is May Day. These are the pleasures that have
brought happiness to man over the centuries.

No sooner had the swallows begun to swoop in and
out of the narrow barn door than Fred became curious
as to what they were up to. He would disappear inside
while Penny, too experienced to be interested in such
matters, remained munching among the buttercups.
After a minute or two Fred would reappear in the doorway, but instead of coming out into the field to join
Penny he would stand stationary, blocking the entrance.
It is possible that this was a deliberate act on his part
to hinder the swallows, more likely it was a ploy to
relieve the tedium of the day. He enjoyed diversions.
His floppy ears almost reached the stone lintel of the
doorway, and his frame filled the rest of the space.
Would he annoy the swallows? Would they twitter
angrily with frustration? He was quickly to find out.
Each swallow dived at him from a height, and flew into
the barn between his floppy ears like supersonic aircraft
between two peaks in the Alps.

Penny, meanwhile, is a lady who enjoys poor health
when she has a chance to enjoy it. Her foot, so the vet
explained to us, had a slight sprain and no more. Yet it

was far too much trouble to walk even a few steps towards us when we brought her carrots and chocolate biscuits. Indeed her interpretation of the role of an invalid was so exaggerated that she would lie comfortably in the furthest corner of the field expecting us to walk to her, kneel beside her, and push offerings into her mouth. This desultory behaviour would naturally have alarmed us had we not had the reassurance of the vet that there was nothing to worry about; and also the added evidence of our own eyes when we saw her, a few minutes after we had disappeared from her sight, gadding about the field like a two-year-old. Ill health for Penny was an entertainment.

The lush period of summer had now begun. Young green bracken was thrusting through the thickening grass, through the mass of leaves of the fading bluebells, draping the sides of lanes and blanketing the moorland, hiding paths which were once easy to find. Coarse docks and thistles sprouted in the daffodil meadows among the dying foliage of the daffodils. Ought we not to be efficient daffodil growers and keep the meadow sprayed with herbicides instead of relying on the motor mower in due course to cut them down? But we prefer to let the wild flowers be free, the good ones and the bad ones, and in June this summer the insects were humming in the meadows, butterflies stretched out their wings on useless weeds, chattering whitethroats clung to the thistles pecking at the first seeds. Up the lane from the cottage the stream had already become a trickle across Monty's Leap, the may tree beyond the gate on the right was a dome of white-scented petals; nettles and foxgloves, Queen Anne's lace, clouds of pink campion and inevitable cow parsley filled the verges and the ditches. And the leaves were now thick on the branches of the elm where the nest of the mistle thrush used to be, and on the branches around the woodpeckers' hole out of which the eldest one, at any moment, would be ready to fly. The window of the bathroom looks out on the donkey field with the wood running along on the right.

I was shaving in the bathroom, looking at my face in an inadequately small mirror, when there was the same hysterical crackling sound that I had heard a few weeks before. It was obvious what was happening, and I glanced quickly out of the window before dashing to the back door. Sure enough, I saw through the window that two carrion crows and the jackdaws were fighting over something up there on the electricity pole; and by the time I got through the door and had run into the field, clapping my hands and shouting, the fight had become a din; and it only became silent after they saw me, after they had dropped with a thud the object they had been fighting over, after the jackdaws had hurried away, after the carrion crows, cawing, had left for the far part of the wood.

The object was our young woodpecker. They had watched and waited and caught him on his first flight.

This summer we grew two and a half thousand tomato

plants, and we chose a type called Moneycross and another called Maascross because both these types tasted like true tomatoes. This age of uniformity has cast its spell on tomatoes like everything else; and this summer it was officially decreed that when tomatoes reached the shops each pack must contain tomatoes of the same size. No mention is made of flavour. If the shape fits the grade, the tomato can taste of soap or of nothing at all; and so the housewife, oblivious of the pressure directed upon her buying habits, comes to believe that a neat, uniform plate of tomatoes on the table is an emblem of wise buying. It happens, however, that the tomato varieties most used for uniformity have no flavour; top grade they may be, and of exquisite shape, but they are tasteless.

Jeannie and I soon lost patience with the grading instructions and we devised a means to circumvent them. We decided to have two grades of our own choice; and on the little piece of paper stuck to the container, that officialdom demanded should show the grade code number, I put the figure '2' or the word 'small'. The latter described all the very small tomatoes we sent away, while the figure '2' described the rest. Now by marking our tomatoes as second grade we had an immediate advantage. We were saved from any pedantic complaints about the size and shape of our tomatoes which an inspector might make; the tomatoes had to be very poor standard indeed to be considered third grade. On the other hand we were not doing our tomatoes justice. Hence we had invented a slogan. In bold red letters printed on a card with my name on it, which was stapled to the container alongside the little piece of

grading paper, was the slogan: 'TOMATOES GROWN FOR
FLAVOUR'.

It worked wonders.

Boris liked tomatoes. In fact he liked them so much
that he appeared to behave as if he were a connoisseur
of tomatoes. He was fussy about each one he selected,
and he was not so co-operative as the blackbirds. He
preferred to waddle along a row biting a piece out of
one tomato then another as, in another sphere, an
experienced wine taster sips importantly a range of
wines. Boris never finished, as the blackbirds did, a
tomato he had once tasted; and so he was a menace
when the first truss was ripening because the tomatoes
were easily within his reach. Thus he had to be pre-
vented from entering the greenhouse; and the greenhouse concerned was the one in front of the cottage,
the others being too far away from his normal perambu-
lations.

It might appear that it was easy for us to stop him,
and indeed it was. All we had to do was to block the
lower part of the open doors, the doors we kept open
on warm summer days to help ventilation, with the two
wire-framed trays that we had nearby for the purpose.
Unfortunately we were always forgetting to use them.
Time and again there would be a cry from one of us:
'Boris is eating the tomatoes . . . nobody has put the
trays across the doors.' Then one of us would go in and
tell him that he had to leave; and he would hiss and
waggle his tail feathers, and slowly plod outside. Later
in the season, when the trusses were out of his reach,

we did not have to disturb him if he chose to spend the day in the greenhouse; and sometimes Lama would be there too. Lama curled up in a small black ball, Boris with his head tucked inside his wing. Both sound asleep.

Incidents like these filled our summer days, trivial moments of diversion, the minutiae of living. I would sit on the bridge, staring across the shallow valley, the sea to my right, listening to the sounds that belonged to these summer days . . . pigeons cooing in the wood, a lark singing, a cuckoo in the distance, the flap of waves on rocks, a girl's voice calling in the cows, the chugging engine of a fishing boat, the donkeys' snorting. Yet unimportant in themselves, these passing pleasures posed the question, the everlasting question of the twentieth century . . . has anyone the right to slow down the tempo of his life in an attempt to come to terms with his inner self? Or should he surrender to the pressure of conventional living, accept the tribal customs, sacrifice truth in the pursuit of power, view life as if from an express train?

Most of us conform. We stifle the secret hopes we have for personal freedom but find we cannot kill them. They were with us before we were smoothed by habit; and though sometimes they seem to fade away as the years pass, we suddenly find ourselves faced with them again in the form of frustration. There they are, challenging our weak selves, demanding why we have betrayed them.

Expediency, we reply, we had to earn a living. We became involved in a career, and we were chained to its progress. Or we may be practical by explaining that we never had the capital, never could hope to acrue the capital, that would have made it possible for us to break the pattern of our lives. Or we may admit that we lazily allowed time to slip by. Or we may say that the chance for change never came our way, or perhaps we didn't have the wit to recognise it when it was there.

Yet whatever the reason, the middle-aged of today have an excuse if they believe they have failed themselves. They were caught unawares by the great god efficiency which is the deity of progress. They were passively passing their lives away, vaguely expecting their dreams to be fulfilled in some distant future, when suddenly they were forced to worship this new god, and this god, uncontrolled by any humanitarian definition as to what he should give in return for the upsets he causes, decrees the closing down of old established businesses, orders victims of takeovers to look for jobs elsewhere, forces homes to be sold as a consequence, children to be removed from their schools and the lives of people to be disrupted at an age when they might expect to be consolidating. The efficiency cult can become the human tragedy of the seventies. It is obsessed with the cutting of costs. Nothing else matters; and so quality suffers, and service, and the dignity of individuals.

Meanwhile the middle-aged face the present. Those who have been successful, the ambitious and the power hungry, chase the prizes which beckon them, then find the prizes have turned to ashes when they have been won. Material ostentation, making people jump to obey their whims, living a jet existence around the world, creates a spiritual vacuum, or ill health, or a broken home. Speed has destroyed quiet moments of reflection by offering the successful too many alternatives, too many opportunities. A safety valve is missing. They have no time to contemplate, are scared to do so. Then suddenly the party is over, and they are lost.

The others, the undistinguished and the unimportant, always loyal to their families, leading their conventional lives out of a sense of duty, watch the prices go up, the fares go up, and then are forced to sacrifice another small pleasure which had helped to compensate for the queuing, the sardine travelling, and the noise which dulls the senses. They fear the change which is taking place around them, but are mute. This is progress for the common good so it is useless to protest. They gaze at the monster earth-moving machines clawing at the ground, and watch buildings familiar as old friends disappear into lorry loads of rubble. Nothing is secure. The fields where the Sunday walk is taken are scheduled to be the site of the new housing estate. The road in front of the house is to be widened, and it will demolish the front garden. Only the insensitive can be the winners. Only those who, in the name of efficiency, dictate the orders. And perhaps even they may sometimes wonder whether their own lives have become victims of their own actions.

I sometimes think of the succession of crofters who lived at Minack over the past five hundred years, and envy them. They did not have to compromise as Jeannie and I have to compromise. Sometimes I touch the old rocks around the cottage which they also touched, and the years run away in my mind, and I feel close to these people whose lives were governed by the seasons. Then they believed God was in charge, not governments. They had a natural faith. Simplicity was an uncomplicated virtue taken for granted. Wisdom was instinctive, not a product of theory. Nature crushed them, and exalted them; and they were a part of the world around them as the hares, and the corn, and the wild seas, and badgers on moonlit nights, and the cries of vixen, and haywains, and the swallows coming in spring.

'Heavens,' I said suddenly, 'the swallows are dive-bombing Boris!'

The bridge seems to breed inconsequential remarks. No discipline in the conversation is needed in order to have pleasure. One is watching a passing scene, and this warrants interruptions, or sudden changes of subject: a sudden flight of birds across the sky, a cuckoo calling urgently in the wood, Lama stalking a mouse in the grass by the apple tree, scores of such incidents are considered by ourselves as moments of importance. So now Boris. Boris attacked by the swallows! The old boy was wagging his tail feathers in embarrassment. He had been up to the cottage for a meal of crumbled homemade bread scattered in front of the door by Jeannie; and he was beside the lavender bush on his way back to the grass around his pond when the attack took place.

Swish! One of the swallows missed his beak by inches. Swish! The other swallow skimmed his back. Poor Boris was bewildered.

'The young ones are soon to fly,' I said to Jeannie, then got up and went down the path to walk beside him. He plodded very slowly these days, and stiffly as if he had rheumatism. We had been more anxious than ever about him, although he gave no positive sign that he was ailing. He still had a good appetite. He still flapped happily in his pond. But there was an air about him that gave the impression of age, of a general slowing down of his ways.

'Come on, old Boris,' I said, 'I'll be your escort.'

He hissed fussily as he waddled on. He wanted me to know that he was perfectly capable of looking after himself.

'Boris!' I suddenly shouted, 'they're dive-bombing *me*!'

A swallow had passed so close that I felt the rush of air on my face.

When I was a schoolboy, and at other times in my life too, I have sometimes felt the need to be accepted in some conventional circle whose members seem to accept each other for granted. But such acceptance can never take place. I have felt all my life that members of a group, however worthy of their intentions, are running away from themselves. I believe one has to learn to face oneself alone, to try to come to terms with all the opposites inside oneself. Groups, it seems to me, exist to blur the truth from their members, becoming mutual admiration societies except when jealousy begins to irritate. Groups, in my mind, have always mirrored escapism, not the individual who travels alone.

The gulls objected to the swallows' behaviour. They

considered the attitude of the swallows so impertinent that they would point their beaks to the sky as they stood on the flat top of the chimney or on the rim of the roof, and cry out their views on the subject. All through the year they were accustomed to treat the chimney and roof as their home during the day; and to expect their measured flight to the rocks and back to be undisturbed. Then these upstarts from South Africa who basked in the sun all those months when they themselves coped with the rain and the gales, suddenly started to bait them. It was intolerable. Yet they were powerless to stop the baiting. The swallows would skim over them as they cried, or dart at them as they glided towards the sea. It was easy to realise that the swallows infuriated them; but I have also to be fair to the swallows. The gulls are solemn creatures. I have never thought they had much sense of humour.

Fred keeps a keen watch on any activity on the sea along the Minack coast. He appears to know the regular fishing boats, for although you may find him looking at them you do not receive the impression that he is particularly interested. A strange vessel, and his mood is quite different. Ears alert, nostrils quivering, you can see into his mind ... what's that strange boat doing here? Or he may become fascinated by some craft which has anchored offshore, and although it is probably there for a quite simple reason, there are sometimes exceptions. He was fascinated one summer evening, for instance, by a fishing boat whose skipper was repeatedly blowing a klaxon horn. This was a ready-made situation for query and excitement, and Fred, who was with Penny in one of the cliff meadows at the time, responded as if he were a coastguard on duty. He was quicker to realise the skipper was in trouble than I was. He started to prance up and down the meadow, pausing every few seconds to stare out to sea; and indeed making me feel that if he had a telescope available he would have put it to use. It was a still evening, and the klaxon horn must have been heard over a wide area. So, too, Fred's bellow. He let out one of the loudest bellows in his repertory and it must have echoed over the water to give comfort to the distressed skipper; and it also appeared to have had an even more practical result. Within seconds I saw a distant fishing boat alter course. The combination of a klaxon horn and a donkey's bellow had alerted the crew; and soon afterwards they were towing the boat towards Newlyn.

High summer, and the end is beginning. The elder-flowers have turned into berries, the apples are fattening, the tomato plants have only the top trusses to ripen, the air sings with insect sounds and flies bother the donkeys. Convolvulus is winding up the camellia bush beside the rose garden, up the fuchsia and the honeysuckle in front of the cottage, up any plant or bush it can find; bees fill themselves with honey from the mignonette on the bridge, multi-coloured nasturtiums tumble over the rocks, night-scented stock and tobacco plants romanticise the evenings. There still seems much of summer ahead . . . but the swifts are gathering, briefest of our bird visitors, and any evening they will be spiralling into

the sky above Minack, calling their shrill cry of farewell, higher and higher, until they disappear in the fading light.

I no longer hear the cuckoo. I was walking with Jeannie and the donkeys along the path towards Lamorna when I saw the last cuckoo of summer, three of them, in fact; a before-breakfast walk, and the fishing boats were passing below us, hastening to Newlyn fish market. I saw them perched on the rocks of Carn Barges and for a moment I thought they were woodpigeons. Then I realised my mistake and I called softly to Jeannie and we stopped; and as I did so Fred nudged me in the back, so I put a hand over his muzzle which he knows to be a signal for quiet. We stood there and watched, then away the cuckoos went, flying south. 'Jeannie!' I had called, in a fit of sadness as they took off, 'hold on to their tails!' And we both laughed at my nonsense.

The swallows remained. Our brood still flew gaily together around Minack, playing the games in the sky, chasing each other high above the stable field and away over the green tops of the elm trees, out of sight, and back again, swerving, dipping, twisting; and suddenly they would be tired and they would swoop down on the electricity cable connecting the cottage, and settle side by side twittering for a moment or two; then off again. At night they still roosted in the barn, clustering together on a beam, but they were not to be there for much longer. Their parents shooed them off. The eggs of the second brood had been laid in the same nest, three of them; and when they were hatched, the barn was a nursery again.

And since that night I first became aware of the Pleiades, Jeannie had come into my life; and I had learnt there were no rules to follow in a happy marriage. Only that both of you must feel that you have freedom and that you are not chained to a conventional routine. Habit is what must be avoided. Every day must bring the unexpected so that, in a way, you remain strangers anxious to discover each other. All my years with Jeannie have been an adventure; the frivolous, glamorous times of London . . . or the first night at Minack when we slept on a mattress on the floor while the rain dripped through a hole in the roof. The companionship I have had with her has had its warmth through the unexpected. I am unable to take her for granted. She is elusive, provocative, feminine, always ready to make a sacrifice, showing faith in reality by not running away from it, yet always on the verge of chasing wild, imaginative Celtic dreams. No dullness with Jeannie.

The swallows were leaving. The electricity cable which ran from pole to pole through a gap in the wood, up the valley to the farms at the top, provided the resting place of the travellers from up country. Long lines of swallows would settle for a while, cleaning themselves, twittering, dashing away to skim the fields and moorland, then back again. They would stay for a few hours or so, longer sometimes, and then off towards Lands End and, if the wind was fair, straight on across the sea to France or the Basque country, even a long flight to Portugal. What parts of this country had they come from, what old houses of England had been their homes during the summer? I was saddened by the gay manner with which they were leaving. No British winter for us. We want the sun of South Africa. Let's fly away as soon as possible.

Our second brood, however, were still in the barn; and I had observed that, as always, there was one more advanced than the others, a bossy young swallow with white shirt front, rimming the nest, seizing the best flies brought by his parents. We called him Pip, and the other two shy ones, Squeak and Wilfred. Any day now they would be learning to fly, and they had not much time to spare if they were to be strong enough to start on their journey before the autumn gales began.

My father, when I was a child, warned me never to ask questions about sights that were naturally beautiful. Accept them, he used to say, as a means of exciting your emotions but do not try to analyse why. I do not suppose he expected me to take this advice too literally, but I have learnt to understand what he was trying to tell me. Those who were guided by the heart, he used to argue, were closer to the truth than sceptics who were always trying to satisfy their intellects. Pleasure, in fact, should be for enjoyment and not for critical investigation. An out of date view, of course, in this technological age. Yet it is a view that still has substance for some of us.

At night I took a torch to the barn to check the swallows which were roosting there. The parents were the first to go. Pip went next, five days later. Then Squeak four days after him.

I was never happy as to what happened to Wilfred. He was always the weakest. He still came back to the nest a week after Squeak had gone.

Then he too disappeared; and the summer was ended.

Cottage on a Cliff

Inconveniences can enhance the pleasure of living. We have never bemoaned our isolation because we are cut off from much of the floss of civilisation. Indeed the contrary is true. As civilisation becomes more rarefied, more dependent on watching instant history, more influenced by media personalities offering instant opinions of doubtful sincerity, there is an increasing delight in being primitive.

Michaelmas Day is the beginning of winter. The day when retiring farmers hand over to their successors, when beefy lifeguards have departed from the now deserted beaches and holiday hotels have closed till another summer, when seashore car parks are empty and pampered gulls wonder what has happened; when ice-cream kiosks are shuttered and the winds begin to blow; when some will grumble that life has become too quiet and others will be glad the holiday season is over: 'Cornwall belongs to Cornwall again.' The visitors have gone.

There are sleepy flies on the last blackberries, spider webs stretch across narrow paths, I flush the first woodcock from a patch of battered bracken as I walk towards Carn Barges, a fieldfare in the stable meadow below the cottage looks surprised to be in a strange country, a last wasp buzzes dozily against a window of the porch, blue tits have returned to the bird-table after being self-sufficient during the summer, faded honeysuckle still blooms in odd places down the cliff a hundred yards away, ivy leaves are yellow-green and leaves of the brambles have turned a robin-red. Wild violets are in clusters. Winter gorse is in flower.

I pull up an imaginary drawbridge at Monty's Leap when winter comes. I play a game that Jeannie and I live in a fortress with a deep moat surrounding us. We have no part in the busy, fractious, unsatisfied outside world, and nothing can disturb the easy motion of the day. Strikes, inflation, unemployment, violence, greed, envy, all these I pretend play no part in our lives. I have passing fantasies that peace of mind has been permanently obtained by looking after our own lives instead of interfering in the lives of others. I am therefore immune, I pretend, from the tedious troubles of the herd. I live in a world where time is mine. I am a countryman living in a remote place with the chance to keep my own identity. I am as simply happy as the uncomplicated peasant of a hundred years ago who never left his parish. Such a game I may play for a day, for two, for three, and then some incident will occur which wakes me up to reality.

It was a lovely morning. A morning that belonged to summer. A still sea, soft salty scents, a quiet sky. I could have believed it was a June morning except there were no swallows dancing in the sky or darting in and out of the barn door; and the bracken swathing the moorland was a red-brown instead of a rich green, and spider webs simmered on the hedges, and the leaves of the elms had begun to fall in the wood, and plump buds were showing on the December-flowering camellia bush. The year was lying about its age. It had produced this Indian summer to fool the Red Admiral butterfly that fluttered from leaf to leaf on the escallonia opposite the entrance to the cottage, and the blackbird which sang a spring song in the blackthorn near the well, and the fox I saw basking in a corner of the field on the other side of the shallow valley . . . fooling also myself, as I walked off to see the donkeys, into pretending no winter lay ahead, no storms to prove again the omnipotence of the elements, no misadventures.

The donkeys were reliable watchmen, and their hearing was as acute as their eyesight. I have seen them many a time look up from the grass they were grazing, then stare intently into the distance with ears pricked; and in a minute or so I would find someone coming down the lane, or observe a figure moving in the moorland far away.

I have a dream, a muddled dream, that I live in a city again. I dream that I live in a featureless room above a car-filled street tied to a job I do not enjoy, enduring the day instead of living it. I press buttons on a cunning machine which I do not understand; and I am confused because at one moment I am obeying the orders of my company, the next of my union. Then suddenly in my dream I become affluent. I find myself imprisoned within conventional success, an important executive who is living expensively, winning applause from superiors, experiencing temporary triumphs, finding macabre fun in playing with power. A glossy, restless, hard-working, sophisticated life which provides the spur for beginners.

Then comes the end of my dream, and I am frightened.

I suddenly see myself as a disembodied person who is observing and taking no part in the action. And I see a countryside as it was many, many years ago when it was free from man's calculated interference. There are crooked fields with the hedges still intact, and lanes sided by an abundance of wild, useless beauty, lush vegetation, butterflies, weeds, insects, no sprays or insecticides to kill them. Horses plough the fields, and foxes and badgers roam wooded valleys living in earths and setts which are only known to a local or two. New motorways do not threaten them, nor the giant, roaring, clawing machines intent on laying waste the land for the benefit of the factories and beehive housing estates. The sea is clean, and rivers are crystal clear. There is no sour sight in this romantic dream. And yet at the end of it I am frightened.

We were to have another creature that winter, staring at us through the glass. A racing pigeon who had tired of racing. At first we took little notice of it as it hung around the neighbourhood of the cottage, sometimes huddled on the roof, sometimes perched on a jutting stone in the building we call a garage, sometimes squatting on the grey chippings while Lama watched it from a distance. For the temporary presence of a racing pigeon was not unusual. Racing pigeons, wayward racing pigeons, like to pause at comfortable homesteads if they find themselves in the mood. Maybe a young bird has lost its way, and needs a rest to regain its nerve; or perhaps it is an old bird, now cynical about the purpose of racing and expending so much effort. In either case they do not normally stay long, a week or two at the most. Then off, refreshed, flies the young bird to search for his distant loft; and the old bird, resignedly, sets off for his.

Nellie, at first, was just another pigeon who would soon be off and away, and we paid no more attention to her than was our habit towards itinerant pigeons. We gave her grain and water, made some remark when we passed her, and waited for the day when she would no longer be with us. Gradually, however, as the weeks went by she began to impose her personality upon us, and impose it on others as well ... Lama, the gulls on the roof, our local chaffinch, robin, blue tits, and the dim little dunnocks. All of us became aware that we were in the company of a Presence. I began to find myself, for instance, stopping to talk to her, instead of passing her by with a casual remark. I felt she expected me to do so, and I did not want her disapproval. Her attitude towards Lama was equally compelling. Lama, who at first treated her with polite curiosity, was startled to find Nellie behaving in a bold, challenging fashion towards her. Lama, curled in a niche of rock sheltered from the wind by the porch, dozing, would suddenly wake up to find Nellie advancing towards her ejaculating: 'Coo, coo, coo!' ... as if she was meaning: 'Boo, boo, boo!' The small birds received similarly provocative attention, and they soon found it unwise to attempt to snatch a grain or two from the handful we had scattered on the ground for Nellie; for she would dart at them in greedy fury. As for the gulls on the roof, their lazy dignity was made to look foolish when Nellie, in a dashing sweep from the sky, decided to join them. For no valid reason she would jostle them away from the spot they had chosen to survey the scene below them; and, except for Philip, they would surrender their positions without argument. Philip, our oldest gull on the roof, would never budge. He would stare at Nellie, then open his wide beak. Nellie never made the mistake of testing his intentions.

Inconveniences can enhance the pleasure of living. We have never bemoaned our isolation because we are cut off from much of the floss of civilisation. Indeed the contrary is true. As civilisation becomes more rarefied, more dependent on watching instant history, more influenced by media personalities offering instant opinions of doubtful sincerity, there is an increasing delight in being primitive.

Winter had now become a companion. In the wood I found nests which I had not seen in summer. The bushes and trees were bare, and I suddenly discovered the tiny nest of the goldfinches who had haunted me in June and July with their bell-like chirruping, and darting red and gold. There it was in the hawthorn just above me as I passed Boris the drake's old hut, clusters of red berries now around it. A few yards away, within touching distance of the path, was a thrush's nest hidden in summer by the green leaves of the blackthorn; and cupped in the fork of another hawthorn was the nest of a chaffinch; and in the bank close to a magnolia was that of a robin; and in the ivy that greedily climbed an ash-tree was a bundle of moss belonging to a wren; and in the branch of a willow were the dried sticks of a woodpigeon's nest; and in one of the elms was the perfectly rounded hold of a green woodpecker who never stayed to use it.

Winter unmasked summer. Summer had hidden the various things I had forgotten I had left in odd corners of the wood where I had left them year after year, each year intending to remove them until the year had gone and summer had returned, and I had done nothing. Discarded pieces of wire netting now matted into the ground. Rusty sections of cloche frames. A battered, galvanised water trough for chickens. Jam jars now filled with compost from old leaves. The rotting roof of the chicken house, covered by ground ivy, in which Queen Mary, the Rhode Island Red who came with us from Mortlake, hatched her only chick. The bottom half of a broken hoe. A strand of barbed wire. More wire netting, and the stretch was still there against which Lama dashed hysterically when she was a wild kitten, trying to escape from the chicken run while I ponderously attempted to catch her. I touched her then, for the first time, and then away she ran, up a tree, on to the hut roof, a leap to a branch, down to the ground again, and out of sight. The wire netting served no purpose now. We gave up the chickens long ago and the hut, since Boris died, had only been used for the storing of fertilisers and other cumbersome goods.

This winter, I said to myself, the wire netting must be removed, so, too, the other tangible memories of the past. I must not be fooled by the lush greenery of another summer.

Black clouds emptying their rain, were scurrying across the bay like upside-down mushrooms. At intervals the sun broke through, shining like a brilliant dagger on the sea. This was a sea that was glad of the turbulence to come, waves were slapping each other, leaving trails of foam in their wake, and watery pits; and above, yet so close that they seemed to be playing their own idea of Russian roulette, were the gulls. They dived at the waves, and swept through the spray; and settled, settled on the surging mass, bobbing spots defying the mountains which seemed at any moment to smother them. This was the beginning of the storm, the limbering up; and in an hour or so the gulls would have gone, gathered on sheltered rocks or inland fields, heads crouched in feathers, facing the wind, leaving the sea to rage.

I went out and braced myself against the rain and the gale, and strode to the gate of the stable meadow, a chewed wooden gate, made so by the donkeys when they were bored by the absence of attention; and I passed through the gate, passed the donkeys themselves as they stood, bottoms to the hedge, heads down, tolerating the storm with a dopey attitude of patience. Yet the barn door was open for them. They had only to move there and be out of the wind and rain, but no. They desired to indulge in donkey masochism. They preferred to maintain the donkey tradition that they were a persecuted race.

On I went along the path, across Fred's field, down to the little gate at the top of the cliff, down the steps, down through the pocket meadows, past the palm tree which I planted when my mother died, through the narrow gap between two hedges of blackthorn and into the bottom daffodil meadow of all, then down again to the point where the grass ended and the grey rocks began. Here was my journey's end. Here I stood with the grandeur of a Cornish sea just below me, watching it foaming the rocks where we lazed on summer days, watching the great waves mounting their assault, coming nearer and nearer, and growing, and the tops curving and sharpening so that for a split second the tops resembled a knife's edge before they thundered down on the rocks which halted them. This was a scene which belonged to immortality. I was seeing the same waves, hearing the same roar, wet with the same spray, nothing had changed throughout the centuries. This was the universe. This was the back-drop to all history, to all conflicts between nations or individuals, to impatient ambitions, to the passing fashions of each age, to the vanity of man. This was continuity which some ignore, some deride; and in which some find comfort. Man's conceit as he over-populates, drowns the countryside in concrete, pollutes the sky and the rivers, will surely wither. One day he will learn the universe is master.

Only the elements, we thought, would be our enemy; and when in due course we endured gales which pulverised our crops, or a sudden frost which destroyed six months' income in a night, we were comforted by the knowledge that nature had been the architect of our defeat, not man. Nature represented freedom, and could be forgiven; man, in contrast, offered chains, and more chains. Man's mistake is to believe that freedom is orderly.

Jeannie once imagined a joke method of measuring

happiness. She invented in her mind an instrument called a happometer, designed on the same principle as a car milometer or a walker's pedometer, except that it was operated manually. Her idea was to measure each moment of happiness during the day by pressing a button on this happometer; a touch for a flash of happiness, a long touch for some out-of-the-ordinary happiness. Thus a business tycoon might push long and hard at the button after a successful takeover bid, a politician perform the same after rousing an audience to hail a policy which gives him some personal kudos, and Jeannie would celebrate in the same fashion because, perhaps, she had been thrilled by the dying evening light on winter bracken, the sea beyond; or the delight of an unsolicited purr from Lama.

Nellie had her independence.

When the rains came day after day, when cold winds blew, when snipe rose, zigzagging in front of us as we walked up the lane to fetch our milk from Walter and Jack's farm at the top, when owls in the wood hooted messages on frosty nights, when fluttering flocks of linnets, finches and starlings raided a field then another, when summer snails were asleep in crevices, when the donkeys preferred to shelter in the stables and we ourselves were glad to be indoors beside the fire, Nellie behaved as if she was impervious to the weather.

She continued to settle on the glass roof of the porch from time to time during the day; and when we threw grain to her on the ground, she was as bossy as ever towards the blue tits who tried to have a share. She was vociferous towards them. She burbled insults and threats, then she would make a dash at one who was proving to be too bold; and when the grain had gone, she would follow us as we walked by expecting more. She was attached to us, that was clear. She liked our companionship, liked to observe the comings and goings of Minack, liked the way we took care of her; but she remained aloof. She had no intention of becoming a pet bird. We were a convenience, no more. She had no wish for us to touch her, and she was expert in evading our attempts to do so. And even in the stormiest weather, she always flew away at dusk.

January. Grey seas and skies. Bare trees. Snipe piping. The screech of a water rail from the marshes near the reservoir. The pile of logs lessening. Yellow patches of winter gorse amid battered brown bracken, shining like lamps. Gunshots. Plovers rising into the sky, wailing. Winter heliotrope scenting by Monty's Leap. Puddles outside the porch door now that the snow had gone. Nellie as hungry as ever. The tits, a chaffinch or two, the dunnocks, and the family of house sparrows clinging together like gypsies, all begging for the bird table to be filled. Majestic gannets flying south a mile offshore. The hum of a distant tractor. White camellias on the bush by the rose garden. The scented mauve flowers of the veronica.

A Cat Affair

*An old countryman, like Walter, is caught between his
proved contentment in the way of life of his past and
the necessity of being on the bandwagon of twentieth-
century progress. Any countryman, for that matter, is in
the same trap. He distrusts city-type standards, yet seems
to have little power to resist them. The cement-based
apostles of progress have a charisma which the countryman cannot match.*

'What are you looking at?' Jeannie asked.

A warm, late October afternoon, and we had taken
our saucerless cups of tea to the terrace close to the

cottage we call the bridge, where Jeannie and I often sat or stood watching, absorbing the antics of birds, or a fox, or the changing colours of light, or the passing of the seasons, green bracken, brown bracken, flattened bracken, wasting time by watching.

'There's something black in the corner of Bill's field,' I said, 'over by the hedge on the right. I thought it was a carrion crow at first.'

'What is it, then?'

'I need my field glasses.'

'I'll fetch them.'

Jeannie ran back to the door of the cottage, passing Lama curled like a black cushion in the cup of an old rock, one of the rocks which formed the foundation of the cottage. A rock which had been there since the beginning of time, solid witness of history . . . Athelstan, Middle Ages, the Spanish Armada, Marlborough, the loss of the American Colonies, the Bastille, the Prince Regent and Beau Brummel, Trafalgar, William the Fourth and the Reform Bill, Melbourne, youthful Queen Victoria falling in love with Albert, the unorganised emotions of the Brontës, the Great Exhibition, Oscar Wilde, Mafeking, Edwardian grace, Bleriot, Passchendaele, Marconi's first message across the Atlantic, horses leaving the land, old values fading, jumbo jets pencilling the sky, ocean liners discarded, cement, motorways, over-population . . . the rock where Lama curled was the same as in the beginning.

I now looked across the narrow valley to Bill's field and to what I thought for a moment to be a carrion crow; and I now saw clearly that I was watching a black cat.

'A black cat,' I said to Jeannie, 'which is about to jump.'

Its body was quivering, paws were shuffling to gain the feel of a comfortable springboard, a mouse was about to be its victim, then a leap . . . and failure. Too soon or too late I would never know, because all I could see was a spread-eagled posterior, and obvious frustration.

'Let me have a look,' said Jeannie, and I handed her the glasses.

'He's pretending it never happened. He's found a tuft of grass to be interested in.'

At that moment, if I had known it, the step had been taken that was to change our life at Minack.

And that of Lama.

I can imagine the people who lived their lives at Minack pursuing the languid journey from birth to marriage to death, uncluttered by the side issues which fill, or empty, the society of today. They were enjoying, and quite unselfconscious that they were doing so, a natural life.

These ghosts of Minack have left their impression. I sense their presence. How, I sometimes wonder, would they face the problems which Jeannie and I face today? For, although we may still possess the kind of freedom which is denied those who are forced by circumstances to lead routine lives, we are aware that the theorists are catching up on us. We have become, like everyone else, units in the national computer, and we are now the servants of Mr Average; and we no longer can sentimentally pretend we are isolated from the herd. We gaze wondrously at statistical reports and discover what we do. We play bingo twice a week, place *Crossroads* at the top of the charts, eat more bananas than we did two years ago, go less often to football matches, drink more beer, and are unfulfilled because we have no telephone in the house.

Such examples of Mr Average may seem trivial, but there is an underlying significance about them which is disquieting. For the cult of Mr Average fools people into believing that we are all equal; and we are not, whatever the politicians and union leaders may say. The bleat of fair shares for all is as futile as the expectation that all horses, hacks, hunters and selling platers have an equal chance of winning the Derby. We can't all be a Gauguin or a Churchill or a Mozart or a Nicklaus or a Jane Austen or a Margot Fonteyn.

Yet the mood of this age urges us to be indignant if we are not, or to be full of self-pity; and the result is a barren philosophy of envy which leads people to believe that rewards come as a right, and not as a consequence of talent, luck, and endeavour. The cult of Mr Average taunts us to disregard ourselves as individuals. Our contrariness, our complexity, our special likes and dislikes, our subtle emotions which often surprise ourselves, are ignored when the computer does the work. It only seeks one result . . . the materialistic Mr Average.

Walter Grose is the third farmer at the top of the lane, and for many years he was tenant of yet a third farm which spread out from the higgledy piggledy buildings, but after Jack Cockram came along they joined up together in partnership. Walter, a bachelor, however, did not live at the farm, his house was in St Buryan village, and he used to travel to work by van early every morning and return late at night. A long day among the fields and his cows . . . and his cats.

He had numerous cats which lived around the farm buildings, black and white cats, cats with brown smudged faces and brown and white bodies, patchy grey cats; and, of course, numerous kittens, half grown cats and somnolent elderly cats. They waited expectantly for his arrival in the morning, then gathered around the van as he produced their breakfast; and they gathered around his van again when he had his crust, when he had his dinner, when he had his tea. Walter was a Pied Piper of cats.

I came up the lane one April morning at the time of our first new black cat alarm, and saw Walter bending down, fingering the leaf of Hart's Tongue fern which was growing in the bank. This fern is named after the tongue of a fully grown deer, and it is pale green, delicate in texture, with slender tongue shaped leaves.

'Lovely,' he said, without looking up, 'man couldn't make anything as lovely as this,' then added, 'never, never take nature for granted.'

An old countryman, like Walter, is caught between his proved contentment in the way of life of his past and the necessity of being on the bandwagon of twentieth-century progress. Any countryman, for that matter is in the same trap. He distrusts city-type standards, yet seems to have little power to resist them. The cement-based apostles of progress have a charisma which the countryman cannot match. The countryman, rich in the minor matters of life, has no persuasive answer to those who demand more land, more land, and still more land for housing estates, motorways, schools and factories. The countryman watches the badger setts, home for a thousand years of badgers, demolished within the hour by a monster machine; or that of a fox's earth, or the site of a long used heron's nest, or hedges and undergrowth where warblers, chiff-chaffs, whitethroats make their nests after flying thousands of miles to do so. But what arguments can he produce to prove that the preservation of such minor matters is more important than yielding to the materialism of the human race?

'When I was young,' said Walter, 'we went looking for plants like these, and wild flowers, and there was excitement in finding them. It wasn't just a few who did this; most of us felt the same way.'

'You didn't have the advantages, Walter, of television and cars and motorcycles.'

'What advantages? Are they happier racing back to watch a programme than I was finding a patch of wild violets mixed with primroses?'

One March morning I came out of my office which used to be the stables, and was faced by a startling sight.

On the near side of Monty's Leap was crouched Lama. On the other side was a black cat.

They looked at each other sleepily; and they were both identical in size and shape.

They reminded me of book-ends.

I hurried over to the small greenhouse where Jeannie was packing the bunched daffodils. It is a job that requires concentration, and Jeannie does not like being interrupted. She counts each bunch that she is packing in a box; and I often address her at these times, and she does not answer.

'There's a black cat the other side of Monty's Leap, and Lama is this side. They're staring at each other.'

Jeannie was not listening. She had to pack perhaps a hundred boxes a day, and each box had to be perfect.

'There's a black cat the other side of Monty's Leap,' I repeated.

In order to keep the bunches in place during the journey to market, a horrid metal rib is lanced into each side of the cardboard box over the stems of the daffodils; and do it carelessly and you can cut a finger. Jeannie safely completed this task on a box and then, as if she had suddenly come alive to my presence, turned round to me:

'What did you say?'

The maddening thing about the situation was that the new cat had infiltrated into my mind. He had touched a soft spot, my awareness that loneliness is pitiful whether a human suffers it or an animal. Against my will I had found myself from time to time thinking about him; and I was moved by his perseverance which he had pursued without brashness. This black cat did not have the trustfulness of a Felix. He wasn't barging in on our lives. He was hovering on the perimeter, watching, nervous; and, except for the occasion when he chased Lama round the corner of the cottage, he had done no harm. I had a hazy interest in the cat, like that of a man who wants to know a girl better when he shouldn't.

'I was thinking of Oliver.'

'Why Oliver?'

'After Mike.'

Mike Oliver was a friend of ours who kept a cat and dog home near Newquay.

'All right . . . Oliver.'

The donkeys have their own special moods. Fred's mood, for instance, sometimes fits him into the role of Coastguard Fred and at other times of Security Guard Fred (when he trumpets a warning that a stranger is about) or of Huntsman Fred (when he chases a fox cub across the field); and during the summer there are often opportunities to be Greedy Fred.

I am sure Coastguard Fred is his favourite role. He is fascinated by shipping.

The most spectacular moment in Coastguard Fred's career, however, will surely be the occasion when the *QE2* paid a visit to Minack; and he was able to answer the deep, rich sounding siren of the *QE2* as she passed a mile or two offshore, with his personal hoots. He was hysterical with pride and pleasure, a pinnacle in coastguard watching experience; and his photograph with Penny beside him, and the *QE2* so close that she seemed to be touching their noses, was published round the world. The only two donkeys who have ever received a salute from such a liner.

The occasion had its beginning when the legendary Captain Warwick, first of the *QE2* captains, wrote to us one July saying that he would like to pay a visit to Minack, though he would have to bring the *QE2* along with him. The *QE2* at that time was calling at Cobh in Eire on her way home from New York to Southampton, and her route normally took her south to the Scillies; and so a diversion to Minack would be comparatively easy.

Captain Warwick had asked us to put up a signal to mark our exact whereabouts; and so we had borrowed the pole which Jeannie used to prop up her washing line, and fastened to it a gaudy orange tablecloth. We then stuck this temporary flagpost between two boulders at the edge of what is now forever called the *QE2* field. The photographers then asked us to stand by the flagpost with each of us holding a donkey, and it was at this moment that things went astray. We couldn't catch the donkeys. We had let them loose because we believed they would become restless if we kept them on their halters too long.

We chased the donkeys round the field, and this they thought very amusing. They threw out their back legs as they passed each photographer, barged over a tripod belonging to ITV, and laughed their heads off as Jeannie and I panted after them. At last they were caught, new white halters fastened on them, and all four of us arrived at our flagstaff. It was a few minutes before five.

The field we had chosen had a clear view of the sea, but it was hidden to the west by a shoulder of land thick with bracken and elderberry trees. Thus, from where we stood, we could not see the *QE2* approaching down the coast from Land's End; and we had to rely on a sentry. The sentry was Geoffrey. He posted himself at a spot where he could see the *QE2* sail into view, and we agreed that he would shout as soon as she came into view. This he did, then hurried back to join us.

We waited . . . then suddenly, as if she was coming out of the bracken, she slowly appeared, a mile offshore. I was overcome by her beauty, and the contrast of her modernity against the wild, primitive setting she was passing. For a thousand and more years sailing ships had passed Minack, and had been watched, and commented upon; and now this lovely liner, the last of the luxury Atlantic liners, was greeting two donkeys. The deep siren, the donkeys lashing their tails and hooting in reply . . . and Geoffrey's Cornish voice behind me:

'She would make a good wreck.'

Oliver continued to haunt Minack, and we continued to ignore him. It was not too difficult to do so because he never, until one day in late September, crossed to the cottage side of Monty's Leap. He would sit for hour upon hour beside the granite post of the white gate, staring up the lane as if he was willing us to pay him attention. He certainly was not begging for food, so he was no doubt having enough from somewhere. Yet what compelled him to come to Minack despite our rebuffs?

The rains fell, and Oliver did not mind.

He made himself a niche in a pile of old grass and bracken trimmings which was heaped beside the lane just beyond the Leap and the white gate. Above it were the bare branches of an elm and a may tree, and they gave him little shelter. His shelter, for what it was, was a small umbrella of bracken covering the dent in the grass on which he curled. He might be there for two or three days, then away for the same period; and if we walked up the lane he would lift his head and stare at us as we passed, an intent though timid stare.

At the beginning of December I found him lying there at night, and, though the sky was clear, a gale was howling through the trees, and a small branch fell in front of me as I walked. His unusual faithfulness had begun to get on my nerves. We were conducting a war with a cat who refused to be defeated. There we were ignoring him, refusing to feed him, and yet by a Gandhi-like meekness he was putting us in the wrong. Now, having seen him lying there at night, I began to doubt whether our toughness was justified. Something compelled him to behave in this manner, what could it be? I had no answer to this at the time, though I felt the moment had come when he might have a reward. One had to be pretty heartless to ignore such remote control devotion. It didn't seem foolish to offer him again a saucer of milk.

Jeannie laughed when I suggested it.

'After all these weeks of sanctions, you give in!'

'Sanctions never are of any value,' I answered, 'if the opposition is determined.'

Soon he had another victory.

'There's an old wooden box in the barn,' Jeannie said, 'and if I put it down there near where he's sleeping, and put some straw in it, he'll have some protection from the weather.'

Oliver moved in the same day without any encouragement from us. He was there on Christmas Eve, then absent during Christmas Day, but back at nightfall when Beverley Nichols paid a call on him.

That night an easterly was blowing, and we put on coats before walking down the lane to visit Oliver in his box. I carried the torch, Beverley a saucer of chopped turkey, and Jeannie a saucer of milk. Oliver was about to have a feast, and we only hoped he would be there.

He was there all right. I shone the torch towards the box, and lit the pinpoints of his eyes. But would he answer our calls? Would he respond to the most inveigling noises that Beverley and Jeannie could devise? Certainly not.

Like Lama, he was immune to flattery.

'All life,' I said, 'except this instant, is a dream.'

'Why do you suddenly say that?'

'Well,' I answered, 'what do you remember of this morning?'

'I got your breakfast, the post came, I wrote a letter to my sister, I wrote half a page of my book . . .'

'All hazy now in your mind.'

'I suppose so.'

'That's what I mean. Half one's life is dreaming of the future, the other half dreaming of the past.'

'I understand.'

'Our sophisticated years are now a dream, all the times at the Savoy, a bottle of champagne on ice in our room, a first night . . . Cholmondeley House, Thames Bank Cottage, glamorous parties in your office with Danny Kaye and all the others. Only the instant was permanent.'

'Like now.'

'Yes . . . you and I and Lama, and that robin, and the gull sailing down into the bay, and that wave moving in to smack the rocks . . . this is the instant which is real.'

Jeannie laughed.

'And now it's over!' she said.

There was no easing of the rain and the wind in the morning. The cottage windows are small, too small for present-day building laws, and so when the clouds are low it is dark in the sitting-room. It was very dark that morning, and we had our breakfast with the standard lamp switched on.

I finished breakfast, and went over to my desk and

picked up a pipe and filled it. But I paused before I lit it and looked at the rain lashing against the window, the window from which I could see the barn and the lane leading down to the Leap.

'I think,' I said suddenly, 'that before I do anything I will go and see how Oliver is getting on.'

'I'll come with you . . . I'll take him the fish that Lama's left.'

We reached the Leap, and the stream was a yard wide and gushing towards the sea; and we half jumped to cross it, and a few yards on we came to the spot in the copse beside the lane where Oliver's box was placed, and found it awash.

'Idiots,' I said, 'we should have remembered this gully was sometimes flooded.'

No sign of Oliver. No sensible cat, in any case, would remain in a place where there was no shelter. If Oliver was wise, he might have had dreams of a nice warm Aga, and given up his siege of Minack. That would have suited me. I would like to be rid of my twinge of guilt.

'I'll leave the fish here in any case,' said Jeannie, her voice almost inaudible in the noise of the storm.

'Better not, it'll be drowned in the rain.'

So I took the saucer from her, and we started back to the cottage.

On the other side of the Leap, a few yards up on the right and close to the little land-well which is covered by a stone canopy and where past inhabitants of Minack once filled their pails during the winter, is a gorse bush. It is a large gorse bush with gnarled branches and dense prickly foliage, and in early spring it has a resplendent display of yellow scented blooms.

We were about to pass it when we heard a miaow. A sharp crack of a miaow like the sound of a rocket fired from a boat in distress.

We both darted to the gorse bush . . . and there was Oliver crouched on a wrist-wide branch three feet from the ground.

'Oliver!' Jeannie cried out, and I added, 'Couldn't you have found a better place to be in this weather?'

The daffodil season that year was enhanced by the presence of Fran. Fran was an Australian girl from Burnside, Adelaide. She was just twenty-one, fair and small, sturdy, affectionate, occasionally moody, indefatigable and very willing; and she had a wonderful way with Geoffrey.

'Get a move on, Geoffrey,' would sound the Australian accent as they went out together to pick daffodils.

'It's just not good enough, Geoffrey,' would come the Australian accent again, 'you shouldn't leave things hanging around like that!'

Fran was on a working tour of Europe. She had been in this country a few weeks and had a job in the Co-op in Reading when her sister, with whom she was staying and who had come to live with her husband in England, proposed that she should write to me. They had read a book or two of mine. Fran wanted to see Cornwall . . . and she preferred the outdoors to a shop counter. So the two of them concocted a letter to me; and before I had time to answer it, Fran one Sunday morning arrived at our door.

'Couldn't wait,' she explained, 'to find out whether you wanted me.'

She had arrived in an ancient two-seater car, had driven from Reading, and it was January, and the forecast that morning said heavy snow was on the way. I said she was welcome to work during the flower season, and we fixed a date when she could come, and I said I would ask Mrs Trevorrow whether she could stay with her.

'In fact I'll ask her,' I said, 'whether you can stay there tonight. You can't drive back to Reading with snow coming.'

'Oh yes I can.'

She spoke defiantly. Why is it there are those who grate when they speak their mind, while there are others who give no offence? I took Fran's attitude without concern.

'See you on 21 February,' I said.

'Sure.'

I first saw them together one afternoon in late summer, a few hundred yards down the lane between the farm and the main road. They were sharing a gateway into a field. Oliver at the hinge end, his lady at the other; and there was a gentle adoring look on Oliver's face which showed no change when I called to him from the car as I passed. The lady was not pretty. She was brown, black, grey, white, with a slash of orange across her face; and though I believe most people would pass her by, Oliver was enraptured. Several times afterwards I saw them together, and the mood between them was always the same. They were deeply in love.

At the beginning of October, I saw the lady at the Minack end of the lane, close to Monty's Leap. I am sorry to say I hissed at her. I also shuffled my feet hastily on the gravel so that the noise frightened her, and she ran away. Oliver was causing trouble enough without also having to cope with his girlfriend. After this incident she disappeared, and I did not see her again.

In the middle of October, however, an event occurred which was one of the strangest I have ever known in my life.

It was a Sunday morning. Jeannie had taken the car to St Buryan to post letters and to collect the Sunday papers; and after she had left I strolled down the lane to Monty's Leap.

Oliver suddenly appeared as I stood there and, with the confidence he now had gained, came up close to me. As he did so I heard a tiny cry in the undergrowth to my right from the direction of Oliver's box we called the Wren House. An instant later I could not believe my eyes.

A tiny ginger kitten, the exact colour of Monty when he was a kitten, stumbled out of the autumn leaves which had gathered beside the lane.

And Oliver ran towards it, and began immediately to lick it.

I left them together, Oliver licking the kitten as if he was the mother, and hurried up the lane. Jeannie would soon be back, and I had to stop the car before she reached the gate, and tell her what had happened . . . and warn her that we would have to get rid of the kitten forthwith.

'Stop!' I cried.

I had reached the well, halfway up the lane to the farm when I met her. She looked bewildered. I had never before confronted her and the Sunday papers in such a fashion.

'Bad news?' she asked anxiously.

'Terrible news,' I replied, 'Oliver has brought us a kitten!'

The engine was ticking over. Jeannie's side window was down, and I was appalled to see her face mellow into gentleness. No sign of shock. No sign of disapproval; and I realised I had been an idiot to expect from her any other reaction. Her record provided enough evidence that she wouldn't be on my side.

'Well,' I replied, 'it is a very odd situation. There I was standing with Oliver by the Leap when there was a miaow from the undergrowth just beyond the gate, then out on the lane appeared this tiny ginger kitten.'

'Ginger?'

'Yes, ginger. That's the extraordinary thing.'

As it happens I never called Monty ginger. I described him, after I had first met him playing with a typewriter ribbon on the green carpet of Jeannie's office at the Savoy Hotel, as the size and colour of a handful of crushed autumn bracken. I could have described Oliver's kitten in the same way. I didn't do so to Jeannie because it might have suggested enthusiasm on my part.

Then she saw the kitten.

We had reached within twenty yards of Monty's

Leap, and there in the shadow beside the lane were the two of them. The kitten was nudging Oliver.

'It's Monty!'

The damnable part of the situation was that I couldn't argue with Jeannie. The kitten *was* Monty as I remembered him as a kitten. The little white shirt front, a smudge of orange on each paw, a tail with dark rings against cream, the rings graduating in size to its tip. There was only one difference, and an important one at that. Monty, on that afternoon at the Savoy Hotel, immediately set out to woo me by endearing antics. His double, so many years later, behaved in exact opposite fashion.

As we approached, he fled.

'Now Jeannie,' I said, 'we have to think of Lama. No soppiness on your part.'

My tone was a mistake. I sounded aggressive, anticipating a mood which I knew was there but which was not yet on display.

'I'm not being soppy.'

'I know you're not, I didn't mean that, but you know how you *can* be . . .'

'*You* found the kitten, *you* were standing by Monty's Leap . . . I wasn't.'

My intentions were good, but I had manoeuvred myself into being in the wrong. This can easily happen. One slip, and the other is at you. You try to retrieve yourself, make a counter-blast, and before you know where you are there is an argument over a matter quite different from what you began with.

She was laughing.

'You *do* get unnecessarily worked up sometimes,' she said. A remark I could not deny.

'My apologies,' I said, making a mock bow. Then jokingly added: 'Nevertheless I'll leave you if you feed that kitten.'

The kitten, after a few weeks, had to be given a name; and as Jeannie is a natural name giver I left the task for her to do. The first step was to discover whether it was male or female; and so, since it was impossible to catch it during the day time, one night we stole down to the shelter with a torch. I put my hand into the bedroom, seized a wriggling ball of fur and held it up while Jeannie investigated. It was a boy.

'Ambrose,' exclaimed Jeannie almost immediately, the torch still shining on him, 'we'll call him Ambrose!'

'Well,' I said, letting him escape from my hand, 'what a very odd name for a kitten.'

'It's simple,' she explained illogically, 'when the torch lit up his face it softened the ginger colour of his fur, and it looked amber. Then his little face made me think of the amber musk rose in the garden, and so I put two and two together and there's the name Ambrose . . . Amber-Rose. See?'

We were walking back to the cottage, and she couldn't see my face in the dark. I was smiling tolerantly.

Later I was to learn of another Ambrose, a St Ambrose who lived in Italy in the fourth century. He was a distinguished lawyer who became a Roman Catholic priest and a great preacher; and he took special pains to attack the dogma of the Roman Catholic church that animals have no souls, that man alone is a spiritual being. This dogma, he believed, resulted in great cruelty being inflicted on the animal world; and he preached a series of sermons which were published in Italy, urging his hearers to treat animals with kindness, and as part of the oneness of life.

'What is it,' I said to Jeannie, my eyes on two gannets offshore, 'that we most value in our life here?'

The gannets dived, disappeared for a second or two, then reappeared, flapping in the water, gorging their fish. Then up they went majestically into the sky.

'The taste of freedom in its purest sense,' she replied.

I knew what she meant. Freedom was once governed in this country by common sense, just as behaviour was governed by conscience. Laws were then limited to guarding the framework of freedom and these laws were respected, just as the rules of behaviour were respected. Of course there were abuses, but the offenders had to risk the moral condemnation of their comrades, and intangible punishment which hurt. Today there is no such condemnation. We have become instead bemused by cynicism, and by the overwhelming mass of legislation which, although enacted in the name of freedom, is eroding it. Freedom is no longer synonymous with fair play for the conscientious, the loyal, those with pride in work well done, and the man who cherishes his chosen way. Instead, in this affluent age, freedom relishes the chip on the shoulder and the couldn't-careless brigades, blackmail of the public by striking minorities, high wages without responsibility, obliteration of the corner shop and the small farm, and a creeping destruction of the values which aeons of time have proved to be the base upon which our inward happiness depends.

Thus when Jeannie said 'the taste of freedom in its purest sense', she was thinking as Emily Brontë was thinking when she roamed the moors above Haworth, mankind and all its chains banished from her mind; the glorious awareness that there are dimensions in living which wait to be discovered by those who are prepared to discard their man-made prejudices, open their eyes and ears, and have the patience to be quiet. Quietness is the secret. Quietness opens the door to sensitive pleasures. The noise lovers will never understand them, never know them. They may see, but they will not feel.

On occasions we have to go away; and one such occasion loomed in front of us not long after Christmas. We were invited to stay at the newly built Berkeley Hotel in Wilton Place off Knightsbridge for its opening party, the last, probably, of the truly luxury hotels which will ever be built in London. And one reason for the invitation was, of course, Jeannie's past position in the luxury hotel world . . . her book *Meet Me at the Savoy* was the story of her life as public relations officer of the Savoy Group, and her novel *Hotel Regina* was described by a BBC reviewer as 'incomparably better than Vicki Baum's *Grand Hotel*'.

Thus the years she has spent at Minack, helping to dig potatoes, weeding anemones and violets, cooking in the tiny cottage, her clothes becoming green as she tended the tomato plants, shoulders growing tired as she heaved the daffodil boxes . . . had not checked the top professional hoteliers from knowing her worth. She might live in the country but she would never adopt provincial standards. She had a sophisticated hotelier mind, and this was recognised. *Gourmet* Magazine of New York, for instance, had recognised this and had proposed she could go anywhere she liked and write for them (the Berkeley was one such place and she wrote a world-quoted article about it). But, as far as Jeannie was concerned, most important of all, her one time chief Sir Hugh Wontner, Chairman of the Savoy Group and Lord Mayor of London, appreciated her flair as well. Hence his personal invitation to attend the Berkeley opening party.

The Berkeley was not yet open for ordinary guests and we had, except for one other couple, the whole hotel to ourselves. Nobody else on our floor, or the floor below, or the floor above. It was as if we were Arabian oil potentates. It was as if I had had a mad dream in which Jeannie and I owned a luxury hotel in which nobody else was allowed to stay. There we were a few hours away from Lama, Oliver, Ambrose and the donkeys which at that moment would be munching the grass in the stable meadow . . . and we could press a button, and hotel staff would hurry to fulfil our demands because there was no one else to hurry to.

The opening party was in the evening after we arrived. It was scheduled to begin at six o'clock.

While Jeannie began changing, I rushed into the bathroom for a shower . . . too hastily, too hastily. I turned on the taps, stepped into the bath and stood up. Bang!

I had misjudged the height of the shower, and the top of my head had made contact with the metal spray whence cascaded the water. My predicament was obvious. Twenty minutes to go, and a cut on my head.

'I've cut my head,' I said excitedly to Jeannie expecting sympathy. Jeannie took no notice. I saw she had a needle and cotton in her hand, and the black dress she was to wear lay neatly on the bed.

'I've cut my head,' I repeated. It was most unlike Jeannie not to rush to my aid in such circumstances; and the sight of me standing there with a sponge on my head should have been enough to tell her that something seriously was wrong.

She now had the needle in one hand the cotton in the other.

'A button has come off my dress,' she said.

'Oh, my God!'

Fifteen minutes to go.

'And I can't thread the cotton through the needle . . . please, please will you do it for me while I get on with my dressing . . .'

I screwed up my eyes, held the cotton in my fingers, and lanced it towards the eye of the needle. I missed. I missed again. And again.

'Damn,' I said.

'There!' I said at last and in triumph, 'I've done it!' and handed Jeannie the threaded needle.

She dropped it.

There are times when I am amazed at my patience. I, often an impatient person, can suddenly find myself so serene that a stranger meeting me at such a moment would come to the conclusion that I was constantly phlegmatic.

'Let me try again,' I said gently.

Five minutes left. Needle in left hand, cotton in right, and I lunged.

'I've done it again!'

My cry of triumph echoed around the room. This new, marvellously luxury hotel might echo many cries of triumph in the years to come, but seldom one so triumphant as this. My second threading of the needle had been achieved at the first attempt.

We joined the line waiting to be received by Sir Hugh Wontner, Miss Bridget d'Oyly Carte, grand-daughter of the founder of the Savoy, and Mr Charles Fornara, general manager of the Berkeley. This was their moment of triumph, the years of planning, and the first public presentation of an hotel which would for decades ahead represent the achievement of those who believed in standards, in style rather than uniformity. It was as if we were all present at the unveiling of a genuine picture, instead of a fake.

Unfortunately for myself, the ceiling of the ballroom where the party was held was of glass, and astonishingly beautiful. As the party progressed, however, I was disturbed by the number of people who remarked to me: 'I've just seen your head up there . . . how did you cut it?'

'Lama's getting on, isn't she?'

'Have you still got Lama?'

'She's a good age.'

Age, age, age. The British are besotted about age. If a woman walks down the street, slips on a banana peel, falls and breaks her leg, be sure the press will begin the report: 'Fifty-five-year-old Mrs So and So . . .' Age had to be tagged on to any news. It's a ritual. It had become a ritual to ask Lama's age . . . and I found myself going back over the years and remembering the same questions being asked about Monty. Nothing had changed. The same dismay at the questions, the same sadness, the same stifled awareness that I was blinding myself to the truth. Yes, I knew that Lama was coming to the end of her time and that she would become a black comma in my memory, but I did not want to be reminded of this by such questions. I could touch her now, pick her up, listen to her purr, and I did not want to be told that these subtle pleasures would one day be only a dream.

Such moments of depression, however, were only a shallow layer on the happiness of that summer. There was, for instance, the amusement, and confusion, caused by Oliver and Ambrose. We had already become accustomed to those who excitedly exclaimed: 'We saw Lama coming up the lane!' when, in fact, they had seen Oliver. But Ambrose had never been called Monty until a friend whom we had not seen for many years was startled by the sight of him on the inside window sill of the barn.

'I thought Monty was dead!'

'So he is . . . years ago.'

'I must have just seen his ghost!'

'Can we see Lama?'

Another spring.

'I'm afraid . . .'

Another summer.

'We've come a long way to take a photograph of Lama.'

'I'm sorry but . . .'

Another autumn.

'Is that Lama?'

'No . . . I'll try to explain.'

'What *did* happen to her?'

'She died on 3 March. Just faded away. Nothing that anyone could have done.'

'We heard *Lama* read on the radio in January.'

'I recorded it, recorded her purr before each instalment too. She was all right then, it was easy to make her purr.'

'She had a wonderful life.'

'Yes.'

'So she came to you in daffodil time, and left in daffodil time.'

'Yes.'

'A strange coincidence.'

'As strange as something that happened the evening of the day she died.'

'What was that?'

Sometimes I answered this question. Sometimes I changed the subject, it depended upon whether I thought the listener would be in tune with the magical combination of circumstances which took place that evening.

A gale began to blow in from the sea in late afternoon, and by night-fall a storm was raging around the cottage, the same storm it seemed to me as the night when Lama first cried at the door; and suddenly I heard the cry again.

I left my chair and went over to the door, and when I opened it the light shone on Oliver and Ambrose, waiting side by side in the wind and rain.

A black cat, and one the colour of autumn bracken. As if Lama and Monty had returned to Minack.

Sun on the Lintel

The sense of liberty is a deceptive emotion. We are enclosed in a society which worships the supermarket, and noise, and treats the charm of solitude as a vice. The odd man out is a nuisance and must be stamped upon. We must all be lemmings. We must hide ourselves in groups, hide our individualities, hide our quest for self-fulfilment.

New Year's Day and a black easterly was blowing in from the sea and the Lizard.

'I want you to listen to me.'

'I'm listening.'

From where I was standing with my back to the fireplace, my head level with the great granite lintel which had been heaved into place when the cottage was built five hundred years ago, I could see Jeannie in our galley of a kitchen, concentrating on a recipe book open before her.

'You're not listening,' I said, 'or if you're listening, you're not hearing.'

'I won't be a second.'

A problem of two people being happy together is that they talk too much to each other. A thought comes into the head, and it has to be shared. They are inclined to prattle, gushing their thoughts into words, hoping for instant reaction from the other.

'It's not important,' I said, 'it can wait.'

'I'm ready,' said Jeannie, closing the recipe book, 'what is it you want to say?'

'I want to list my New Year resolutions.'

She laughed. 'How very funny.'

'I'm serious.'

'Oh really . . .'

'All right,' she said, curling herself on the sofa, 'tell me about your resolutions.'

Jeannie is slim and dark, and a mixture of Scots, Irish and English. Sometimes I have clear evidence of the Scot in her, sometimes of the Irish, sometimes of the English.

'Well,' I said, pausing for a moment while I prised out with a matchstick the ash remnants of my pipe into the ashtray on my desk, 'I want to start my New Year resolutions with what I am doing now . . . instead of spilling the ash carelessly on the desk, which it is my habit to do, I'm going to knock the ash cleanly into the ashtray like so . . .'

The ash, with the aid of the matchstick and a knock, fell neatly into the tray.

'That's a good start,' said Jeannie laughing. 'What next?'

'Well,' I said, 'I intend to cook you a gourmet meal.'

'Wonderful.'

'Do you remember that Prunier dish I did one day in Mortlake just before we came to Minack?'

'Years ago, and I will never forget it.'

'Prawns and lemon sole and rice, and the hours I took over the sauce?'

'Sheer artistry.'

'That's the kind of cooking I would like to do again.'

'A great occasion it will be, if it comes off.'

'I also,' I said, 'intend to go through the papers in Labour Warms.'

Jeannie was laughing.

'There are oceans of letters and notes and papers!'

'That's what I mean. It's time we sorted them out.'

Labour Warms was an institution in my life. A massive teak cupboard that was in my nursery in Bramham Gardens, Kensington, then in my nursery at Glendorgal, our one-time family home near Newquay in Cornwall. Then it was installed in my bachelor flat in Elm Park Garden Mews near the King's Road, and later followed me to Cholmondeley House on the river at Richmond, and after that to Thames Bank Cottage at Mortlake.

It was a family heirloom, a reminder of Victorian solidity, of the British Empire at its peak . . . and across the top of the cupboard, painted in blue against the brown of the teak, was the warning:

LABOUR WARMS, SLOTH HARMS.

I have seldom been the person I wished to be, because the person I wished to be changed so quickly that I was unable to catch him. My Walter Mittys have been numerous.

Sometimes I have wished to be a steady, conventional type, playing safe. Sometimes I have wished to live a Bohemian life as varied as that of Augustus John. Sometimes I have wished to be a pianist, sometimes an England cricketer, sometimes an art collector. Sometimes I have wished to enjoy the deceptive applause of transient success, sometimes to run away from it and hide. Sometimes I have wished to be an intellectual, praised by the few, though unintelligible to many. Sometimes I have wished to be gregarious among the sophisticated, sometimes to live the life of a hermit. Walter Mittys have filtered through my life, changing their roles with bewildering rapidity, providing me in their aftermath with many conclusions. Among them is a distaste for those who relish exercising power over their fellow human beings; another is that a fundamental contemporary need is to delve into one's own secret thoughts before becoming anaesthetised by the opinions of a crowd . . . and another is my everlasting gratitude to the Walter Mitty who led me to Minack.

There are, of course, many who would call our attitude to cats a sentimental absurdity. Why bother about the feelings of a cat? Why waste time on animal love when the human race can obliterate itself at the touch of a button; when twisted minds leave random bombs in crowded places; when schoolchildren threaten their teachers with flick knives; when there is a perpetual economic crisis? Animal love, in such circumstances, does seem absurd. It is an irrelevancy compared with the problems of the day. No wonder that pragmatic people condemn animal lovers. Life is too serious for such indulgence.

Unashamedly, however, Jeannie and I allow ourselves such indulgence. Animals offer stability in this unstable world. They do not deceive. They soothe jittery moods. They offer solace in times of trouble by the way they listen to you. They may not understand a word you say but that doesn't matter, because it is a dumb sympathy that you ask of them and they give it; and extra-sensory understanding, which is the more comforting since it is secret. You have no regrets afterwards for having disclosed too much.

Each year when the daffodil season begins we are in the mood of pool investors waiting for the Saturday results. We are always hopeful. We always begin by believing that the combination of circumstances required for a successful harvest will materialise and that, during the few weeks of the season, we will earn the money we have been hoping for all through the year.

The sense of liberty is a deceptive emotion. We are enclosed in a society which worships the supermarket, and noise, and treats the charm of solitude as a vice. The odd man out is a nuisance and must be stamped upon. We must all be lemmings. We must hide ourselves in groups, hide our individualities, hide our quest for self-fulfilment. We must learn to accept the notion that it is naughty to desire privacy. We must make ourselves believe that it is anti-social to have saved for years so that we can be ill in a private bed without strangers prying upon us, that such saving is a sin compared with spending the money at bingo. We must adjust ourselves to these attitudes, and be careful not to challenge them. If we challenge them, we will be given a label and our views will be ridiculed. Yet all we are doing is speaking for liberty and for those who have died, sacrificing their lives for liberty:

> *Went the day well? We died and never knew*
> *But well or ill, freedom, we died for you.*

'The daffs have started,' I said.

'Good, good.'

'Only two boxes,' I said, meekly, thinking of the broccoli and the lorries outside.

'Splendid, Derek,' said Ben Green, in a tone which suggested I had brought in myself a vast load of broccoli. 'Talk to Russ about it. He's the flower man.'

Russ I had also known since our potato days. He was an office boy then, and later a van driver. He was now, as I was to learn during the next few weeks, someone who is unable to terminate a telephone conversation. Thus I would make a visit to Long Rock for the purpose of finding out the prices, and then wait, and wait, and wait, while Russ conducted a conversation with some farmer or far distant wholesaler. On, on, on, would the conversation go with Russ at this end replying in monosyllables while the wholesaler or farmer at the other end poured out his troubles.

Russ was free of the telephone on this occasion.

'Yes, my old cock?'

'Just sent two boxes of Mags to Covent Garden on the train. What's trade like?'

Mags, or Magnificence as they are properly called, are daffodils with a golden yellow trumpet and a soft scent, and they grow in meadows down our cliff, our earliest daffodils.

'A bit dodgy, Derek!'

'But the season hasn't yet begun!'

'A lot of Spalding stuff coming in. Glasshouse stuff.'

I have a letter from my mother which I have never opened. She wrote it to me from London when I was living on an island two hundred miles away from Tahiti in the Pacific; and it never reached me because I had left the island when it arrived. It was forwarded on to me from one address I had just left to another, and another, until finally it reached me months later after I had returned to England. I remember holding it in my hand for several minutes wondering whether to open it and, in the end, I decided not to do so. My reason, I remember, was because the war had begun and the envelope was a gossamer connection with the halcyon days I had lived on the island . . . the envelope had actually *been* to the island. I put it in a drawer, therefore, and as during the coming years I moved from one home to another, I continued to keep it in a drawer. It is here now at Minack. Will I ever open it?

I prefer the white elderflower wine to the red made from the berries and, with its gentle sparkle, it makes a fine summer wine. Picking the flowers is a ceremony, an exciting ceremony because we take the donkeys along to help us, choosing a sunny June morning after the dew has dried from the flowers, and we come down the cliff to the meadows surrounded by elders, and while we pick, using scissors to cut the stems, the donkeys play games. Fred will rush from meadow to meadow, followed by Penny kicking her heels in pleasure, a hilarious demonstration of happiness that they are free to have such a pleasant change from solemnly cropping grass in a field. Then, as we continue to pick, they will suddenly change their tactics and come rushing up to us and nudge us, or Fred will push his woolly face into the flowers. Part of the pleasure when drinking the wine is to remember how the harvest was gathered.

The sun had now broken through the haze and it dazzled a path on the sea, silhouetting the rocks below me, hiding in darkness the gulls that were perched there, so that I heard them squawking without seeing them. Aeons of time and here was the same scene, the same etched lines of the rocks, the same language of the gulls, the same celandines, rose-pink campions, bluebells, wild violets around me, the same greening of the elder trees, the same white of the blackthorn, the same young ferns, the same bridal sprays of the sweet-scented sea-sandwort on grassy banks. A morning to be aware of one's luck. A morning to shout one's gratitude to the heavens. A morning to sympathise with those on trains and buses crowding into cities, or those passing through the factory gates to join the din of machinery. Here was peace. Here was the ultimate which man seeks. Nothing in a supermarket, nothing which could come from the success of a wage claim, nothing that a millionaire could buy, nothing that greed or envy could win, equals the reward of a spring morning on a lonely Cornish cliff, so quiet that you are truly at one with nature, listening to the sea touching the rocks, sinking your mind into unplanned beauty.

I was endeavouring at this stage of my reading to form a philosophy in which I could believe out of personal conviction, and not because it was imposed upon me. I could not accept, for instance, the value of the notion that all men are equal in the sight of God, when it was so perfectly obvious they varied drastically in their physical and mental attributes. It seemed absurd to me that someone who was born to permanent ill health should be considered to have the same chance for a happy life as the man who was capable of breaking the four-minute mile; and equally absurd to accept the cry of 'fair shares for all' when some are born with much talent, and others with none; when there are some who become great musicians, others who remain tone deaf; some who become skilled in their professions, others who are fit only for manual work; some who are scholars, others who are dunces; some who have the flair to organise, others who can only follow; some who have criminal minds, others with integrity; some who are mean, others who are generous . . . I could not accept that the multitude of permutations involving the personality of human beings warranted the belief we were all equal; and that we each had one life; and were then wafted to heaven or hell. The prospect did not satisfy me.

It was unfair; and it was ludicrous to expect the unfairness could be corrected by laws, regulations, and political dreams. The unfairness was fundamental, not man-made. Nor had it anything to do with the environment in which one was born, for history had shown the rich could be dunces; the poor could provide a genius.

I am happier in prayer alone on a Cornish cliff than I am being part of a crowd in a church. For I am unmoved by the mumbo-jumbo of the normal religious services, because they seem to me to reflect an automaton form of worship. The details of the service and the manner of those conducting it seem so contrived that the service makes an artificial impression on me. It has no meaning. My heart is not touched, nor is my mind. I am watching a charade.

Religion for me, therefore, is not a question of dutifully attending religious services of one denomination or another. Religion for me is a secret affair, very personal, and requiring no conventional religious umbrella to shelter under. I do not believe I would be a better person if I read from the Koran every day, or conscientiously attended Communion, or fasted, or lit candles and confessed away my conscience. I could still be a heathen in my behaviour to others. I could still have only a façade of goodness. I could still be a bigot. I could still be a man of violence. The evidence of this surrounds us today. Religious fervour does not bring peace of mind; and peace of mind is what man searches for.

The sun was on the lintel, the massive rough granite lintel above the fireplace. It was no splash of sun. It was a shaft, the size of a fist.

'Summer has begun,' I said to Jeannie, who was in the kitchen preparing dinner.

The sun had moved far enough west for it to be setting below the hill of the donkey field; and as it dipped there came a moment when it filtered through the glass of the porch, through the open doorway, and touched the old stone. Each evening, each week, it moved across the lintel until high summer was over; and then back it would come, imperceptibly moving to the point where we had first seen it, and then it would vanish. Autumn, winter, spring, would pass before we saw it again.

'A warning,' said Jeannie from the kitchen.

'How do you mean, a warning?'

The tiny kitchen is part of the sitting-room, although

it is cunningly hidden; and you would not know it was there unless you looked round the corner over the stable-type door. It was over this door that Jeannie's face appeared. She was laughing.

'A warning,' she said, 'that the year is going by and the New Year resolutions are not being achieved.'

'That's not true.'

'Nearly six months of the year,' she said, 'and you haven't yet fried a sausage.'

'That was never a resolution.'

'Just a joke. I was thinking of the gourmet's dinner you promised; the exquisite cuisine I was going to enjoy after sitting back and watching you prepare it.'

'There was the onion soup.'

'Delicious, the best I've ever tasted, and such skill on your part and patience . . .'

'You're joking again.'

'No, seriously . . . I *am* looking forward to that dinner.'

'Don't worry, you'll have it. There's plenty of time.' Then I added: 'I've done well with the seeds anyhow. That's one resolution fulfilled!'

My resolution to withstand domination by the donkeys was a fiasco, I'm afraid, from the beginning.

I would slip out of the back door if they were in a position to see me coming out of the front, and slip out of the front door if they could see me coming out of the back . . . and then set off on a walk of my own. Or, if they were in the stable field in front of the barn, thus barring my normal route to the cliff, I would go up the

three steps to Lama's field, turn left past the corner where we have built a stone hedge topped with earth and full of flowers, and down another few steps into the *QE2* field. Then I would scurry or, more likely, Jeannie and I both would be scurrying along the top-side of the field until we reached the far end where we would slide down a steep bank into one of our top cliff meadows. We would then believe we were free.

Freedom would be brief. The donkeys' acute hearing would catch the sound of our hasty footsteps or, if they were placed in the right situation, they would catch a glimpse of us as we sneaked away; and thereupon they would set up a heartrending hullabaloo and the sound of it would make us feel sorry for them. After hesitation, and an urgent talk, we would retrace our steps, unlatch the gate, fasten on the halters, and start on our walk again . . . except now there were four of us.

Oliver and Ambrose had been consolidating their places on the bed and, since my resolution banning them from such comfort was now in tatters, I was wise enough to accept my defeat with grace. I was also influenced by the fact that Ambrose was prepared to offer such a sign of affection, because in daytime he continued to be often on edge and elusive. If I saw him outside and went to pick him up, he would still, more often than not, dart away from me; and when sometimes he copied Oliver, turning on his back, displaying his tummy to the skies and apparently inviting me to touch him, he would jump to his feet and run as soon as I was close to him. It was maddening . . . and yet the moments were increasing when tantalisingly he gave me hope that he was changing into a normal loving cat like Monty or Lama or Oliver. One morning after breakfast, for instance, he jumped on to my lap uninvited for the very first time in his life. I was astonished. I sat there immobile, Ambrose overflowing across my lap from cushion to cushion, and called for Jeannie to come and witness such a unique occasion.

The menu was set, a Sunday lunchtime was chosen as the occasion, and the necessary materials obtained. Soon after breakfast on the appointed day, I persuaded Jeannie to disappear from the cottage for the morning; and she went away in a state of apprehension. She could not believe that my Sole Miroton could be anything but a disaster.

I, too, as I stood alone in the kitchen, was in a state of apprehension. My high-sounding promises had reached the moment of action. I had to prepare a fish fumet, and a fish velouté for the Bercy sauce.

> Put four tablespoons of white wine and the same of fish fumet in a saucepan [read the recipe for Bercy sauce] with a dessertspoonful of chopped shallot, and reduce it by a third. Add not quite half a pint of fish velouté, bring to the boil, and finish with two ounces of butter and a teaspoonful of chopped parsley.

Keep calm, I said to myself, read the instructions carefully, don't hurry, and above all don't lose your nerve.

At that moment there was a miaow at my feet.

'Oliver!'

There was another miaow, a squeak of a miaow.

'Ambrose!'

I greeted them as one greets old friends in a moment of crisis. The rush of warmth, the sudden easing of tension. It did not matter to me that they had ulterior motives. I just felt grateful for their presence.

Thus, as I cooked, they watched my progress . . . the stewing of the fish bones, the sieving through a strainer, the making of a roux (flour and butter), the simmering, the preparation of the mushroom purée and the potatoes and, finally, after Jeannie had returned, the poaching of the sole.

'And now,' I said, when I had finished, 'you can be the official tasters.'

And they gobbled a fillet.

Jeannie did not gobble. She slowly savoured my delicacy. She even declared it a triumph of *haute cuisine*. She declared that Sole Miroton was one of the great fish dishes of the world . . . and such was her praise that I doffed my imaginary chef's hat again and again after our plates were empty.

Then came the Cape Gooseberry flan.

And this *was* a disaster.

I set it down confidently on the table, produced a bowl of Cornish cream, and cut two slices. They were uneatable.

In cooking the pastry I had made a fundamental mistake. I had mixed the pastry and fashioned it into the circular tin, but failed to pre-heat the oven. Thus my flan went into a cold oven; and the consequence was pastry which had the consistency of cardboard.

The Winding Lane

Society is so involved in the business of maintaining freedom that it tangles itself in verbal chains, losing thereby the very freedom it sets out to preserve. Freedom, in the old meaning of the word, depended upon a give and take, a moral sense of what was right or wrong, for its preservation. Today, however, our civilisation has become so complicated, our values so warped, political pressure on government so great, that freedom has become an illusion for ordinary people. Freedom is now only a word repeated parrot fashion by our leaders as they rush from making one new law to making another. Freedom has become a mountain of regulations that few can understand.

I do not understand those who say never look back. By looking back the years are not wasted, and one can place the present in perspective. It is too easy to forget the facts, the incidents, the emotions that have built one's life, long ago reasons which determine today's actions.

'Strange how a girl calling like that can make us think,' Jeannie said.

The girl, a young secretary from London, pretty, fair hair to her shoulders, dark blue slacks, a white Shetland polo-necked jersey, had provoked me when she walked down the winding lane to the cottage, and asked: 'Have you lost what you once achieved? Have you lost the first vision?'

People who ask direct questions may irritate, but later you may be grateful to them for stirring the mind. The girl was standing beside the white seat opposite the barn, close to the verbena bush which fills its corner with scent all summer.

'I mean,' the girl went on, 'you have people like me suddenly appearing uninvited, asking you questions, and disturbing your peace, and taking up your time . . . all because of your books about Minack.'

'Well,' I replied to the girl, 'I write about reality. I suppose, therefore, it's natural for people to wish to find out whether this reality is true.'

'About what is a dream for many.'

'An unobtainable dream for many.'

'Why that?'

'Most people are tied to families, jobs, education for their children, or have grown out of the time to take risks, and however much they would like to start a new kind of life, to try to fulfil a dream, it is impossible for them. And there is the cost. Jeannie and I left London when it was possible to live on very little. To start living a life in the country like ours today costs a small fortune.'

I had picked a tiny sprig of verbena while I was talking, and gave it to her.

'It dries like lavender,' I said, 'and always keeps its scent.'

The girl sniffed it.

'Lovely,' she said, her mind elsewhere.

Then a moment later.

'You still haven't answered my first question.'

'About the first vision?'

'Yes.'

'We haven't a telephone,' I said, making a joke of it.

'I suppose you think I shouldn't be asking you these questions, but your books have made me curious to know if you are both still living the kind of life you intended to live when you first arrived.'

Conversations with a stranger can often be less inhibited than with someone one knows.

'People of course have made a difference,' I said, 'but if they take the trouble of tracing our whereabouts, most of them only come because they are on the same wavelength as ourselves. After all, we're difficult to find.'

'No signposts anywhere.'

'And as a result,' I went on, 'we have the experience of meeting all ages, and people from a huge variety of backgrounds, and different countries for that matter, and so we learn a lot.'

The girl was fiddling with her sprig of verbena.

Then again she said: 'You still haven't answered my question.'

'You're very earnest,' I said, making another joke of it. But I added: 'Your question intrigues me. It's just that at the moment I don't know the answer.'

'Are you happy, then?'

'Of course we're happy.'

'You see,' she said, 'so many of my generation want to have a life that fulfils their secret hopes. And we don't know, I at any rate don't know, how we can do so.'

'Nothing new in that. All young generations have been the same.'

I do not enjoy my own birthdays. I do not want to be reminded that the years are passing. I am not in tune with those who proudly announce, like a batsman totting up a score . . . 'I am forty, I am fifty, I am sixty' . . . and then hasten out to celebrate. It is as if nothing has been achieved in their lives except age.

For I prefer to believe that age is an attitude of mind, and that the young can be old, and the old young. Maybe those who have no children have an advantage in thinking this way. They are not made aware of the generation gap in the manner that parents are made aware. They can behave towards children as equals because they have no personal responsibility towards them, and so, as with grown-ups, their relationship with children depends upon sharing a common wavelength;

and one can have a common wavelength with a six-year-old.

A six-year-old came to Minack with her mother, to whom we showed Oliver and Ambrose, and to whom we introduced Fred and Penny (she had a ride on Penny); and at the end of her visit she solemnly called me aside, then proceeded to present me with 2p. Her mother was out of sight, and when I told her she said: 'All Josephine's worldly goods.' I took the coin and buried it in a shallow bed of earth underneath a large rock, and told Josephine, earnest face looking up at me:

'Come back in twenty years and it will still be here where we have buried it . . . and we will call this Josephine's corner.'

Society is so involved in the business of maintaining freedom that it tangles itself in verbal chains, losing thereby the very freedom it sets out to preserve. Freedom, in the old meaning of the word, depended upon a give and take, a moral sense of what was right and wrong, for its preservation. Today, however, our civilisation has become so complicated, our values so warped, political pressure on government so great, that freedom has become an illusion for ordinary people. Freedom is now only a word repeated parrot fashion by our leaders as they rush from making one new law to another. Freedom has become a mountain of regulations that few can understand.

Jeannie and I have never had any inclination to join the

Keep Up With The Jones Brigade. We are, for instance, neither party goers nor party givers, though we both delight in prolonged conversation with a small circle of companions. Parties fragment my mind. Party talk, with its trail of inconclusive sentences, leaves me in a vacuum, and I lose the rhythm of my life, taking a day or two to return to it. I have inquests as to what I have said, or not said, and a vague dissatisfaction pervades me. I find it difficult to concentrate on my task, whether it be writing, or attending to correspondence, or weeding a row of carrots. I am, for the time being, insensitive to small pleasures, the small pleasures which provide the base for happiness in the country. This attitude, no doubt, is a weakness on my part. I ought to be able to divide my life into compartments, cope with social occasions, and then revert to my normal life without ado. But it is not so. Hence I can rightly be labelled an insecure person, that derogatory phrase so often used by psychiatrists. I am, however, glad to be such a person. I would far rather be full of self-doubts than someone who is always sure of himself.

The donkeys were in the field above the cottage, but I always took them down to the field in front of the barn at night. It meant that they could shelter in the barn if the weather became rough; and as dusk fell they usually were waiting for me to take them down, standing side by side by the small wrought-iron gate. I would open the gate, put on their halters, and lead them down the steep gravel path, sometimes with difficulty because Fred would go one way and Penny the other, or both would try to have their fill of escallonia leaves in the hedge beside the bridge, and I would tug them away, calling them to stop, and then suddenly obeying me, they would choose to rush down the path, forcing me to behave as if I had lost control. It was usually a minor adventure, putting the donkeys to bed at night.

I put the halter on Fred, and began leading him to the gate which opened on to the big field overlooking the sea, known as Fred's field because it was beside a rock in this field that he was born. Penny waited behind. She always waited until Jeannie joined her. She had a special affinity with Jeannie, as any animal is inclined to have with one special member of a family. Penny did not have a halter. It was not necessary for her to have one, although we carried it with us in case of emergency, in case she was in one of her ebullient moods. Normally she was quiet and docile, but then occasionally there was this mood when she appeared to say to Fred: 'Let's escape from them. Let's run away on our own!' And if we were not on the alert, she would suddenly barge past us on the narrow path and Fred, who, once through the big field, was also let off the halter, would follow her at speed. Many a time the donkey walk has ended with Jeannie and me out of breath after catching up with the donkeys, by now quietly grazing at some far-off patch of grass, no doubt amused at our distress.

I had been into the field where the donkeys were grazing, for the sole purpose of having a talk with them. I make this sort of visit quite often, not so much to amuse the donkeys as to amuse myself. I feel in need of a diversion, and so I go to the donkeys; and the donkeys, as often as not, will turn their bottoms to me, and continue their grazing. Then, in order to gain their interest, I endeavour to make them play; and an easy way to do this is to take a box of matches from my pocket, run up behind Fred, and rattle it. This sends him off away from me in a spurt; and to keep the pressure up, I run after him, continuing to rattle the matchbox. Often I have played the same trick with Penny; and so an observer, if he happened to be in the neighbourhood at the appropriate time, could have seen me running round the field, the two donkeys racing ahead of a box of matches which I violently rattled as soon as I was within noise-rattle distance to their tails.

One day when I went to the field to play my game I found Penny lying flat on the ground. I urged her to get up with encouraging words. Not a movement. Then suddenly she stirred, slowly gathered her feet under her, and heaved herself into a standing position, and began to inch forwards . . . inch is the word. It almost seemed her hind legs were paralysed.

'Come on, Penny,' I said, putting my arm around her neck. 'Let's go for a walk across the field.'

She inched forwards, then came to a full stop. I was scared.

A while later, three vets arrived, not one. The three of them had been engaged on an operation on a cow in the neighbourhood, and their office had told them about Penny, and they came as soon as the operation was completed.

In the meantime, Penny's situation had changed. It had changed dramatically. No sooner had I returned from telephoning the vet than I saw her walking around the field quite normally. I grew anxious, not because of Penny, but for causing the vet unnecessary trouble when he was so busy. I even wished to see Penny contrive a limp, any gesture I hoped she would make in order to prove that I wasn't just a hysterical, hypochondriacal donkey owner.

She had no intention of helping me. She proceeded to graze unconcernedly around the field, not a trace of discomfort; and the three vets, after examining her closely, pronounced her perfectly fit. But why had she behaved as she had done?

The Christmas Eve mince-pie ceremony was short, only ten minutes, because we always left before the clock struck twelve. Donkeys, according to a tradition, kneel at that moment . . . and we wanted to keep the illusion of that tradition intact.

On this occasion the donkeys came into the barn just as I was trying to light the candle which stands in an old-fashioned candle holder on the ledge of the right-hand window. They had followed Jeannie in, noses up in the air, sniffing the mince pies which Jeannie had on a plate, tempting them by holding the plate just above their heads.

I struck a match, held it against the wick, and had no response. I had not touched the candle since the previous Christmas Eve, for part of the ceremony was that the candle was always the same candle, though becoming lower each year; and I once said to Jeannie that when the time came for a new candle, we would be entering a new era of our life at Minack.

I struck the match again and held it against the wick. Then again. I came to the conclusion that dampness must be the cause of the failure, and a shiver went through me. Why this year of all years should the candle not light? And then on the fourth attempt there was a sudden flare . . . not a simple candle flame, but as if I had lit petrol. It flared for a second or two, then as suddenly died down; and I saw that in a mysterious way the candle had completely melted and, although it was now alight, the flame came from a collapsed candle, a sort of plateau of a candle.

The light flickered, however, around the old barn, and I saw two happy donkey faces being teased by Jeannie . . . a mince pie just held out of reach. Maddening! I saw Penny pushing her nose up, delighted with the game, but thwarted! Of course Jeannie never held out for more than a moment or two; and then followed quiet munching, a shuffle on the ancient cobble floor of donkeys' hooves, and a sense of unbelievable peacefulness on our part.

That Christmas Eve we also had someone else present. I had piled hay at one end of the barn and, in order to keep it away from the donkeys, I had placed an old field gate across it; and on this evening I suddenly caught sight in the candlelight the face of Ambrose, sitting upright in the hay, intrigued by the proceedings, watching us, making me have a thought that he looked like a cherub.

It was a starlight night, and when at five to twelve

Jeannie and I left the barn, I said to Jeannie it was the most perfect Christmas Eve ceremony ever, and she agreed. And then she said, dashing the moment a little: 'Why, I wonder, did the candle behave like that?'

On New Year's Eve we settled down to a quiet evening, then suddenly, there was a banshee cry outside, no hee-haw, no conventional call from a donkey, but a cry of such an agonising note that it sent a chill right through me.

I rushed into the porch and opened the door, and there was Fred, standing there, shouting his message at us that he needed us. Not knowing that the gate was shut (later we discovered he had jumped the four feet drop from the bank beside the gate), we rushed down with the torch to the stable field, and found Penny at the far end lying on her side. She was breathing heavily.

All night Jeannie stayed with her while Fred kept within a few yards, coming close every now and then, nosing her. It was a clear night at first, stars peaceful companions; and as Jeannie knelt there, a rug over Penny, Jeannie stroking and whispering to her, I had dashed off to telephone . . . New Year's Eve and the world rejoicing, paper hats and laughter, and noisy bands, and the singing of 'Auld Lang Syne' . . .

We should perhaps have set out to find another donkey to be a companion for Fred. Many people in similar circumstances would have done so. Two factors, however, stopped us. One was sentiment. Neither of us could bear the thought of seeing another donkey gambolling about the meadows so soon. In time, yes, but for the present we refused to entertain the idea of looking for another. We were impelled to remain loyal for a while to the memory of Penny. It was a form of the old-fashioned custom of going into mourning. It is not a question of going around with a long face. It is just a question of having a pause between the old and the new. No haste to find a substitute for the one who has given you love for years. Wait, and let fate provide the answer.

Sometimes when he was roaming, he would come up the path and round the corner of the cottage to the porch. If we were indoors, we would hear him softly snorting, and we would leap to the door, and welcome him, and find a chocolate biscuit, and if there were no chocolate biscuits, we could cut a slice off Jeannie's home-made bread; and Fred would munch it with enjoyment, and we would talk to him, and stroke his head, and then, when he had had enough both of bread and of our attention, he would turn his bottom to us and wander off. I would watch him, and think what a beautiful donkey he was, the coat of deep chestnut and a way of carrying himself like a thoroughbred polo pony. Heaven knows what his father was like, a hard-working Irish tinker's donkey, Jeannie always likes to think, but both he and Penny shared the very fine characteristics of the traditional Spanish donkey which, in the last century, was introduced to Ireland.

How does one recognise luck when it comes in the form of opportunity? Material luck is obvious, but opportunity tends to be obscure. Hence there have been many times in my life when I have looked back on an opportunity missed, and wondered why I missed it. The opportunity is crystal clear years later, and yet at the time I fumbled, and lost it. Why? If you keep a diary it will help to explain, and I have always kept a diary from time to time but not regularly, because, as Virginia Woolf said, diaries should only be kept at intervals, otherwise the diary dominates the diarist.

A week later I picked up the Donkey Breed Society Newsletter, and I was looking through its roneoed paragraphs when I saw one which caused me to call out to Jeannie: 'We've found him!'

Under the heading 'Donkeys For Sale' was the following:

MINGOOSE MERLIN, large dark brown 18 months old registered gelding, by ROMANY OF HUNTERS BROOK, ex prizewinning mare. Very successfully shown, excellent potential for driving. Kind, knowledgeable home for this exceptionally handsome and lovable donkey my first consideration. Mrs V. Bailey, The Forge, Skinners Bottom, Redruth, Cornwall.

We met Mingoose Merlin over a fence at Skinners Bottom the following afternoon. We were not going to allow ourselves to change our minds, to dither. Fred had waited long enough for a companion, As we set off from Minack we had agreed that Mingoose Merlin was going to be ours.

Nothing fundamental has changed since the beginning. The rocks remain, fishing boats sail past offshore though more silent and faster, everywhere there are yellow flickers of November gorse, the sun glints on rain-wet ivy leaves, gulls float like snow-flakes against the brown-red bracken of Carn Barges, a raven grunts overhead, his November courting having begun, a woodcock zig-zags, there is the thump of a wave on a rock sounding like the slamming of a door, Hart's Tongue ferns peer green from banks, seaweed scents, foot-wide tramped tracks of foxes trace through the meadows, cormorants on Gazelle Point air their wings . . .

Stay still, I say to myself, stay still and make the small kingdom your own. The hustlers see it all in a blur, blind to its inactivities, deaf too, hurrying onward out of boredom, and out of fear of meeting themselves.

'To know the whole process, totality of oneself,' wrote Krishnamurti in *The First and Last Freedom*, 'does not require any expert, any authority. The pursuit of authority only breeds fear. No expert, no specialist, can show us to understand the process of self.'

Stay still, and I see the microscopic details of the kingdom. Stay still, and I am aware of the sounds that I haven't heard before, of the movement of insects that I haven't seen before, and of the wonder in the world that awaits our attention without relevance to the pay packet, or one-upmanship, or the greed for power. Stay still, and I can become aware of my secret self, difficult though it may be. Groups do not give one a chance to do so. Groups, in their gatherings, chatter, postulate theories and solutions, but their members are only running away from themselves. Yet how can one blame them? People require comfort, and group-minded people find this comfort together, particularly in cities where the pace, and the multitudes, deny them solitude; for loneliness is not the same as solitude.

It was as if Mingoose Merlin was coming home, that Wednesday morning when he emerged from the horse-box which deposited him outside the farm buildings at the top of the hill. The gale had died away, the sun was shining, and there was the illusion of a soft spring day. He emerged from the horsebox meekly enough, and, after a momentary pause when he was presented with a carrot, Jeannie took hold of the halter and started to lead him down the winding lane to Minack.

They had gone but a few yards when he began to lead *her*. His trot became faster and faster. She held him all right, but there was no doubt at all that he was in a great hurry. Round one bend, then another, then the straight run to Monty's Leap; and when he reached it, instead of walking through it he jumped, plus-fours in the air, shaggy coat flying; and racing up the side of the barn with Jeannie running beside him, he turned left without hesitation.

And there, waiting at the gate, was Fred.

When the Winds Blow

I have yet to meet a cat lover on holiday who is not worrying about the cat left at home.

I went out of the door, and dusk was falling, and the wind was beginning to stir from the west. I went past the escallonia, night dormitory of the dunnocks, to the terrace we call the bridge, then up three steps into the Lama field, where we grow the Joseph Macleod daffodils, and then turned left until I reached the stone and earth hedge, on top of which I have repeatedly tried to grow a bed of flowers. From here, on clear days, the whole sweep of Mount's Bay can be seen and marvelled at ... and my failure to grow a bed of flowers is unnoticed.

Only Jeannie's catmint has blossomed. The plant came from her green-fingered Aunt Lorna, who used to have a nursery in Bristol and whose plants are in various corners of our garden. The catmint, in due course, became the cats' pub. Ambrose sneaked to it, Oliver adored it ... and that evening in November, when the wind was beginning to stir and I was standing close beside it, the Lizard Light already blinking, the sky above Culdrose Air Station becoming a rose red, factory fishing boats blazing with lights in between, I suddenly became aware of Oliver beside me.

As I stood there, he brushed his head against my leg; but when I, wishing to show my appreciation, bent down to stroke him, he jumped away perversely, up on the hedge, and straight to the catmint. He began nibbling the leaves. That instant, if Jeannie had been with me, she would have said: 'Don't drink too much!' Then, satisfied, he turned on his back, rolling his black person upon it ... just at the moment I was fulfilling the purpose of my coming out of the cottage that November evening. The purpose to watch, unobserved, Fred and Mingoose Merlin in the field overlooking the sea below the hedge, on their first evening together.

Mingoose Merlin's background was impeccable. Jingle Bells, his mother, was a Show donkey; and his father, Romany of Hunters Brook, had appeared in the advertisement pages of the Donkey Breed Society as one of the most sought-after stallions of his time. Mingoose

Merlin, in fact, was a very favoured donkey. It was as if he had rich parents who had sent him to fashionable schools. He wasn't a hobbledehoy like Fred. Mingoose Merlin was registered. There, in the Donkey Breed Society's Stud Book, was written his aristocratic lineage. Fred had no chance at all of being included in such a stud book.

Fred was silhouetted against the darkening sea at the far end of the field, head down, grazing. Twenty yards away, Merlin too had his head down, grazing. In the distance, across the bay, the Lizard Light flashed every few seconds.

I am not sure exactly when our hopes began to go awry. It was a gradual process, but perhaps the first sign was the day when one of the greenhouses, as we moved it from one plot to another, came off the rails. It was not a major incident at the time, because we soon moved it back to its proper position. It was, however, a warning that, after years of use, the rails of the greenhouse had gone out of alignment. First one greenhouse, then another, then another. All showed the same weakness, and as a result we stopped trying to use them as mobiles and used them as static greenhouses instead.

We never lacked advice as to what to grow, or not to grow. The advisory officers of the Ministry of Agriculture were liberal with their help, and it was our fault that we treated them as oracles. This attitude was partly due to our upbringing. The parents of both of us belonged to the mould who, whenever a problem of any kind arose would say: 'Ask the advice of an expert.' It took me years to realise that experts are as fallible as the rest of us but, at the time I was listening to the words of advisory officers, my belief in infallibility still existed.

They were very useful, but I expected too much of them. I am inclined to expect too much of people. I am perpetually turning geese into swans; then I am surprised when whoever it is does not measure up to my expectations. There seems a persistent optimism in my nature which prevents my correcting this fault; and, in the case of the advisory officers, this persistent optimism resulted in my doing them a disservice. Their job was to advise, not to act as managers. It was my job to listen, weigh one piece of advice against another, then come to a decision. If it were the wrong decision, it was my responsibility, not theirs.

It bewilders me that slug pellets are available everywhere, and that they are recommended because they are easier to use than a spray. Slug pellets, unless completely hidden from view, can kill a dog or a cat or a bird. They see the pellets on the ground, think it is food, and that is that. We know of two dogs who were killed in this way.

Independence always poses a problem. People the world over dream of giving up their regular jobs, saying goodbye to managers with whom they disagree, becoming free of the relentless routine of travelling to the office or factory, or of enduring the stress of pressures from those around them. It is a perennial dream for many. Yet, if the step to gain independence is taken, another vicious stress may take its place.

Jeannie and I have experienced that stress in the sense that, for long periods of time, we had scarcely the money to pay for the postage stamps on our letters, and we lived on scrags of meat and vegetables we grew. Yet never for a moment did we ever discuss giving up and returning to the London circle which we had left. Why? Jeannie's perpetual optimism was one reason. Another was that we shared a desire to find values in life other than those to which we had become accustomed. Surface values are fun to enjoy in spurts, but to live with them permanently leads one into a disquieting vacuum. Life runs away and there is nothing to show.

The values we were looking for were those which help to achieve piece of mind and, in our case, they were composed both of negative and positive values. The negative values from which we wished to be freed included the weariness of being with people who mocked sincerity, people who relished intrigue, people who smiled to your face while planning to cheat you, people who considered simplicity a fault, people who were immune to other people's feelings . . . all ingredients of the rat race.

The positive values, on the other hand, which we set out to gain, are more difficult to define. One is in the position of a lover of Mozart, trying to explain the subtleties of a Mozart quartet. Many will be for ever deaf to those subtleties. Many, and I am one, will slowly become aware of them just as I slowly became aware of the multitude of subtleties that have enriched our life at

Minack . . . like the evening when Oliver was with me and I watched Fred and Merlin, and he followed me down the lane to the greenhouse field.

When we were dressed, we went down to the stable meadow gate, picked up the two halters which I had left lying on the hedge, and called: 'Donkeys!'

There was, in fact, no need to call Mingoose Merlin. He came scampering towards us as soon as he saw us approaching, head down, black legs flying, with all the excitement of a puppy. He stood quietly as we opened the gate, then, just to be perverse, he turned and rushed away.

'He's very pretty,' said Jeannie.

There was a thick fringe on his head, thick enough to half cover his eyes, so that one felt one should brush it back if he was to see properly, as one does with an old English sheepdog. His coat was long and the texture soft and would need, I realised, much grooming. His legs, however, were the most surprising part of him because they were so stocky, not due to the bone structure but to the quality of coat which covered them, resembling old-fashioned plus-fours and, to add to this strange appearance, was the contrast of his tiny hooves; hooves which reminded me of a ballet dancer's shoes compared with Fred's clodhoppers. He was a delight to look at, and I could understand how, young though he was, he had been a prize winner at various shows: best foal at the Penzance Agricultural Show; best foal at the Devon County Show; sixth in the national 'Mare with Foal' class at the prestigious Stoneleigh Show. It con-

cerned me that, with such a record, his show days were over.

The bottom meadow was some fifty yards from the rocks, the blue elvan rocks which edge the sea, and there was undergrowth in between; and so, unless Merlin had gone berserk, he could not have made a way through the undergrowth to the rocks. Yet, I was apprehensive.

We had turned the first corner and had begun the descent to the bottom when both of us, simultaneously, gave a shout.

'Merlin!'

He took no notice. He was standing halfway down the cliff, sideways to the path, ears pricked, back arched, looking a worthy reminder of his show championship days. He was quivering with excitement.

A mile offshore, the white-painted *Scillonian* was sailing by on her way to the Scilly Islands.

Merlin had seen his first ship.

From that moment, the onion cliff became the Merlin cliff.

I am perpetually aware of the conflicts within myself. I have been aware of them ever since I drew away from the conventional standards of my youth ('Always be nice to servants in other people's houses' being the astonishing advice of my housemaster when I left Harrow), and I was helped by reading writers who had involved themselves in living full lives. I found no comfort in academic writers and philosophers; no inspiration from intellectual theories as to how youth should struggle for fulfilment, or how youth should attain experience. Thus, only writers who portrayed the realities of life, the subtle tensions which seem so often to be in opposition, who wrote about characters with whom I could identify, writers who seemed to reflect my hopes and fears, who suddenly flashed light into a corner of my mind . . . only writers such as these fascinated me; and, of these, two stood high above all the others: Marcel Proust and Somerset Maugham.

My young life was so predictable, so inhibited by ropes of conventional thinking that I was conditioned into believing that life was a straight road of good or evil, of good manners or bad. There were no side roads, no alleyways. Everyone was judged by their outward behaviour and, if they did not measure up to their expected behaviour, they were shunned. No allowance was given for inner conflicts. No forgiveness offered to those who strayed into an alleyway.

I have yet to meet a cat lover on holiday who is not worrying about the cat left at home.

'I was thinking,' I said, after Merlin had given me another nudge in the back to tell me to walk faster, 'that most of the basics which make up happiness are corny.'

I had spoken, looking ahead, and Jeannie behind me, behind two donkeys as well, only heard a mumble.

'Speak up. I couldn't hear.'

'Most of the basics of happiness are corny.'

'And what does that mean?'

'Telling other people how to live their lives is an industry . . . politicians, the media, academics, intellectuals, the churches, they are all part of the industry. And to keep the industry prosperous, they drench the public with their theories, confusing the public, leading them away from the obvious.'

The donkeys had stopped. A clump of out-of-season campion was being devoured.

'Go on.'

'The theories have to be complicated ones to keep the industry on the move; always promising results in the future, material or spiritual . . . and the obvious is ignored.'

'Which is?'

'The obvious revolves around the corny qualities of love and kindness.'

We were moving again and nearing Carn Barges, where we turn right and start on the final homeward stretch.

'You see, that's what I mean. Happiness is based on corny virtues. That is its weakness. It is too simple for this complicated world . . . and it provokes giggles. Some people are always ready to giggle at simplicity.'

I heard the laugh of Jeannie behind me.

'As simple and corny,' she said, 'as taking two donkeys for a walk along a cliff!'

A crisp, January morning; frost up country, but none at Minack since winter began. The wind is our enemy, our perpetual enemy. Frost makes darting attacks, ice on the water butt that has melted by noon. Frost is not a perpetual enemy like the wind; nor is snow. Frost and snow flirt with us; but when, year after year, we are lulled into thinking that the flirtation is harmless, they will suddenly cause us dismay. The pipe from the well is frozen, no bath water, no drinking water, and I have to take a pail to Monty's Leap and scoop from the stream. Twice, only twice have we been snowed up . . . the lane, drift deep, a white river between us and the farm at the top of the hill.

No prospect of snow on this crisp, January morning; no prospect of frost. It is one of those clean Cornish winter days, when the horizon is clear and the sea sparkles in the sun and the gulls float above the cliffs, and early wallflowers scent their yellow petals. Down by Monty's Leap are the sprawling Ascania violets, and Charlie the chaffinch sits on a fuchsia branch close to the bird table, calling for his favourite sunflower seeds. And up on the roof, a respectful distance between each other, Ronald the rook and Philip the gull wait to scramble for whatever it is that Jeannie chooses to throw to them.

A crisp, January morning and the time for a stroll up the winding lane with Oliver and Ambrose and, as we strolled, we were aware of one special advantage of the life we were leading. No stress to be endured travelling to work, travelling back home. No pummelling in tube trains, no queuing for buses, no traffic jams, no din. We had experienced these discomforts and now we were free, but it was a freedom which could never be taken for granted. Hence when we strolled up the lane with Oliver and Ambrose, we thought of those in the trains, buses and traffic jams and had what may seem to be a strange wish; that each of those who hated their daily travel could miraculously, always on their own, transport themselves to the winding lane.

Animals for me represent a form of anchor in my life; a reassurance, a symbol that in this world of envy, greed and humbug, innocence exists. Such a sentimental summary may not meet with approval. This functional age despises sentiment. It always surprises me that violence is accepted as a way of life, but not sentiment. A hint of sentiment, and it will be met with smirks. Violence, on the other hand, in plays, films, literature, whether in the role of mental or physical cruelty, is lauded. I suppose this is because violence is easier to mirror than sentiment. It is easier to shock than to soothe.

The snag is that when one is self-employed, it is not just the hours one puts into the work that are at stake. There are the capital sums involved. And there are many people who, at a bold moment in their lives, have decided to throw away the security of a dull, remunerative job, for the wide open spaces of independence, and have invested in some project which, after the first great enthusiasm, begins to be a tyrant. It is like being black-mailed. The more you pay, the more is demanded of you. Jeannie and I have had this experience at Minack and as a consequence we were on guard. We were not going to allow ourselves to be under strain. We would not fall into the trap of being over-conscientious.

Within a few years, market requirements had gone from one extreme to another. Not so long ago, the daffodils were forced into full bloom and a bud in a bunch was forbidden. Then began the period when growers were urged to send them in bud, but with a touch of yellow showing; and now there was this new revolution of marketing them looking like grass.

We had enough buds to fill two daffodil boxes, forty-five bunches in each box, ten buds in each bunch and when, before putting the lids on, we looked at the neatly packed rows, just a touch of yellow showing from most of the buds, we felt confident that we had picked them at the right stage. They looked like grass, true enough, but at least there was a hint of yellow.

We were wrong.

From the salesman in Covent Garden to whom we had sent the two boxes came a message with the invoice a few days later. Just two words:

'Too open.'

Too open . . .

From that moment, the moment the invoice arrived, we debated the matter no further.

We surrendered.

'If they want grass, they will have to have grass.'

'Poor wooers,' said Jeannie.

'Never mind the wooers.'

She looked pensive.

'What are you thinking about?'

'I was thinking,' she replied, 'of errant husbands arriving home late for dinner with a bunch of grass in their hands.'

'Be careful . . . so easy to cut yourself.'

Quiet over Christmas, quiet over the New Year, quiet to within a week of marketing the first daffodils, and then a gale.

'Be careful . . .'

Jeannie's advice was sensible, obvious in fact, but I too had to be sensible; and as the gale blew, as glass shuddered, cracked, opened up gaps in a greenhouse, allowing the wind to sweep in, to churn inside, providing the opportunity to create the damage of a miniature cyclone, I could not stand by and watch.

'Be careful . . .'

And I went outside with her words in my ears and the gale in my face, coming from the east, from the Lizard, coming viciously across Mount's Bay.

I had to be sensible. I could not let the capital we had sunk into the greenhouse disappear just because I had to be careful. I had to try to save them. I had to plug the gaps of broken glass. I had to take risks.

One is born, I suppose, with a lack of self-confidence, for no reasoning can expel its mood. Some conduct their lives as if they have never had any doubt as to their abilities, creating an aura around themselves which earns a respect that is undeserved; and there are, of course, those whose self-confidence *is* deserved, who sweep through life with *élan*, never doubting their talents, and these are the lucky ones. As for myself, born with a lack of self-confidence, I belong to the group who shout in the dark, who sometimes brashly pretend the fates are on their side or, in contrast, yield too easily to opposition . . . but the undercurrent is always the same. One is yearning for encouragement to banish doubts.

I suppose I should hate gales. They have done enough damage to us in our time. Potato crops ruined, daffodils flattened, garden plants blackened, summer leaves of the trees turned brown, and always the threat of smashed glass. But I find there is a certain comfort in the fury of a gale, a kind of antidote to the artificial standards of our civilisation. Here we are in this period of technical brilliance, a period in which scientists aim to conquer the natural forces of nature, in which academic doctrines lead us to believe that all will be well with our lives if we follow the rules they expound for marriage, for health, for social problems, a period in which standardisation has become the nirvana, a period in which we are fooled into thinking that there can be fair shares for all . . . and along comes a gale. It lashes the land and boils the sea, turning ships into cockleshells, mocking man's conceit, reminding us as we listen to its roar that man-made theories do not control us, that nature remains supreme. I find solace in a gale. I find solace despite the fact I am scared of the damage it might do.

Merlin, since he arrived at Minack, had been developing various special interests. One of these interests concerned the interior of the cottage. Since it is a small cottage, the size of a normal town flat, the presence of a donkey inside it provokes anxiety. A lamp may be knocked over, a vase of flowers, china ornaments or photographs standing on the oak chest. All these were in danger when Merlin decided to enter the cottage; and he decided to enter each time I was supposed to be leading him from the donkey field, which is above the cottage, down to the stable field or meadow, which is below the cottage. As we passed the short path leading to the porch, he would tug at the halter, leading me towards the porch. Once there, he would walk through the door as if he were walking into a stable.

Of course, it was my responsibility that he performed

this party trick. I could have held on to the halter. I could have pulled him away. But, in the pre-daffodil time, when there was no hurry to the day, I found his desire to look around the sitting-room irresistible. He would walk up to my kidney-shaped Regency desk and push his nose into the untidy pile of papers that lay on it, and he would have a look at the wastepaper basket and momentarily think it contained fodder to eat. There was no hint of clumsiness in his behaviour, only his inquisitiveness was the danger.

Meanwhile, Fred would stay at the door, his head peering into the porch, making whinnying noises, wondering what Merlin was up to, wishing to join him, but scared that his bulk would cause problems if he did so. A two-year-old might be at ease investigating the inside of a cottage, but not a grown-up donkey like himself. I think too, that he was jealous of Merlin; jealous of the attention that Merlin was receiving out of sight of him. Like the moment when Merlin put his head into our galley of a kitchen.

'Merlin!' cried Jeannie, 'get out of my kitchen!'

A wail of whinnying notes from the porch.

'Merlin!'

Merlin had seen newly-baked buns on a plate.

More whinnying notes from the porch.

'Go away, Merlin . . . you're not going to have one here. I'll give you one with Fred outside.'

It was clearly an improvised roof, and so, when I invited a roof expert to have a look at it, inviting him to give me an estimate as to the cost of its repair, the expert gave a snort.

'Don't know how it's lasted so long . . . the wood is rotten . . . look,' and he poked his stick at a plank on the garage roof, 'the wood is soft as sawdust.'

The planks rested across four oak beams.

'The beams are solid enough,' I said, hopefully. Against the beams were still glued the remnants of last summer's two swallows' nests.

'You'll have to cut down that climbing rose before any repairs can start,' the expert continued, ignoring my remark. 'And those brambles at the top end, they'll have to go.'

'I understand that.'

The brambles grew out of the bank. The climbing rose, a lovely white rose which began blooming in clusters in June and continued spasmodically to bloom until the autumn, had lodged its tendrils under the felt which covered the roof, prising it up, splitting it in places.

'It's going to be a big job,' said the expert, dubiously. 'Just as well start from scratch.'

'How long do you think it'll take?'

The expert had brought out a ruler and had begun measuring.

'You see,' I added, 'I am anxious about the swallows. They're on the way now from South Africa, and they'll be here in less than a month, and it must be all ready for them when they arrive.'

The expert stopped measuring and turned to me in astonishment.

'Swallows?' he said. 'Do you mean you're doing all this just for swallows?'

I wonder why I react as I do towards episodes such as the arrival of the swallows. Why should I have felt concern as to whether or not they had a dry roof for their nests? It was such a trivial matter; as trivial as the pleasure I had when Oliver suddenly appeared and joined me in a stroll down the lane, or when I watched Ambrose sitting on the granite rock beside the white seat in front of the barn, resembling a miniature lion as Monty once did; or when I had the fun of watching Fred and Merlin racing around a field. All apparently trivial, yet not trivial to me.

Perhaps my reaction is due to a nostalgia for the friends of my youth. Perhaps I am identifying the innocence of animals with the innocence of my friends who were killed in the Hitler war. My friends possessed an innocence which let them believe that it was worth dying for the cause for which they were fighting. Their innocence let them be convinced that the future, a calm, contented future, enjoying the basic values, was in their hands. If the war were won, their sacrifice would not be in vain. I ponder about my young friends who were killed, as I stand in a meadow staring out to sea, or look at a wild violet or a primrose, or hear a robin sing, or am aware of anything that shares the innocence of my friends who were killed. Cynics will smile at my thoughts. Political activists, deaf to a robin's song, blind to a primrose, will stand up on their rostrums. Sacrifice? Risk being killed? Fools that they did not belong to a union which demanded danger money before battle.

Innocence, in these rushing times, is becoming a lost virtue. Innocence is an ally to magic. Innocence does not spoil wonder by analysing it. Innocence is the acceptance of the unexplained. It offers trust and respect, offers pride in work conscientiously carried out. Innocence enables you to believe that miracles are possible. Innocence means good manners. It is without guile, envy or hate. Innocence is a victim of the materialistic society.

There are days during the winter which the Cornish describe as a day lent. It is a day that, during a period of stormy weather, is serene. A day like a summer day, soft, a haze on the sea, a day that causes the birds to break their silence and sing, a day that makes you forget the yesterday of rain clouds billowing in from the south, the shape of up-turned mushrooms, forget the rush of the wind through the trees. Such a day was a Sunday in late January and, in the morning of that day, I went for a walk to the Merlin cliff, the cliff meadows where Merlin first saw the *Scillonian*. I had walked quite a distance along the path when I heard a miaow behind me, and it was Oliver. I stopped and he came to me and rubbed his head against my leg and I had a special welling of love for him.

'Oliver,' I said, 'how people would laugh at me for loving a cat as I do you.'

A day lent . . . I sat there on the blue elvan rock with Oliver purring on my lap, my mind far, far away from wrecks and stormy seas. There was no logical sequence in my thoughts, I was in one of those rare, hazy moods when my mind is unaffected by immediate problems and you find yourself roaming over a multitude of haphazard ideas which come welling up from the subconscious . . . compassion, which is free, is becoming a rare gift . . . one looks back, cursing oneself for one's mistakes, but forgetful of the climate in which the mistakes were made . . . the generation gap is created by parents . . . one throws a tennis ball (of friendship, of conversation, of an idea) and the receiver muffs the return . . . my generation is kept perpetually young by the media's obsession with the Hitler war . . . sensitive people can understand the philistines, but the philistines will never understand the sensitive . . . in a permissive society it is humbug to condemn prostitutes . . . people, happy in their personal pools, do not wish to be disturbed by outsiders who awake latent emotions . . . luck, at some stage, is a necessity for success . . . laws, aimed at improving human relations, will not force people to love each other . . . intellectuals are embarrassed by emotion . . . why should the majority wish to go beneath the surface of life? Gimmicks titillate and help them get through the day, for this is the throwaway age, materially and spiritually . . . faith in economists and brilliant academics is like believing in Santa Claus . . . the magic of two people meeting for only a few minutes, but who seem to have known each other all their lives . . . there can never be a just justice for all . . . too much knowledge takes away magic, and magic provides the excitement of life . . .

BBC radio announced trees down over main roads and power lines down and areas blacked out. At 3.45 p.m.

on Saturday afternoon, as I was trying to escape from the roar outside by watching a race meeting on television, the programme was interrupted by a warning that weather equivalent to a cyclone was expected in Devon and Cornwall, resulting in structural damage. No sign of snow here . . . but in Devon, Somerset and Dorset there was the worst blizzard in thirty years, with Taunton, Exeter and Lynmouth cut off.

Wait, wait, wait . . .

We sat cocooned in the cottage, reading, pretending life was normal.

'Oliver's off his food,' said Jeannie.

'The storm has put him off it.'

Jeannie was over by the storage heater, tempting Oliver with freshly cooked coley.

'Come on, Oliver. This is good for you.'

But Oliver turned his head away.

Wait, wait wait . . .

We went to bed early, ear plugs again hiding me from my fears. Then up on Sunday morning prepared to find the Orlyt greenhouse a crushed mass of broken glass. We went to look together.

'It's still there!'

The side, forty feet of it, was still swaying in the wind, much of the glass smashed, but miraculously the roof was still holding.

'Jeannie,' I said, holding her hand, 'it's going to survive!'

All through the morning, all through the afternoon and into the evening, the winds continued to blow . . . until at nightfall, as if a tap had been turned off, there was a sudden stillness.

Our world seemed at peace again.

The Orlyt was patched up, polythene sheets draped over it, pending full repair; and on the green bolster, their favourite place in the greenhouse, Ambrose huddled close to Oliver as he had done so many, many times before. They were warm there in the sun.

The vet had come on the Monday after the storm was over, and he had come several times since. We were expecting him again any minute. Oliver was suffering no pain, his life was just ebbing away; and in our hearts we knew that this would be the vet's last visit.

As I waited, I remembered that first time I saw Oliver, in the corner of the field on the other side of the valley which we now call Oliver land; and I remember too, that Sunday morning when I stood by Monty's Leap, and out of the undergrowth appeared the tiny ginger kitten.

I wondered, as I looked at the two of them, how Ambrose would manage on his own.

The Ambrose Rock

I recognise the dreamers because they are the vulnerable ones. They come within the category of the insecure, those whom personnel managers describe as non-executive material. They are those who have romantic fantasies and expectations. They are those who will understand without you laboriously having to explain.

Ambrose followed me into the cottage out of the rain, a wet ginger sponge; and walked over to the space beneath my desk, and began to lick the wet away.

'Come over here,' I said, sitting on the sofa; 'let me dry you.'

He ignored me.

'Come on, Ambrose . . .'

He continued to lick.

'Come on . . .'

Jeannie appeared from the tiny kitchen.

'Won't you ever learn,' she said, 'that you can never persuade a cat to do anything it doesn't want to do?'

'I was wanting to make a fuss of him.'

'I understand.'

It was early March and the daffodil season was at its height, and I had just returned from taking the daffodil boxes to Penzance Station *en route* to Covent Garden. The last sending of the week, for it was Friday afternoon.

'Many going away?' asked Jeannie.

'Too many. Tomlin's lorry was ahead of me, and Le Grice's horsebox, and the lorry from that huge Manaccan grower whose name I can never remember . . . I should think the market will be swamped.'

The sun shone the following week, day after day.

'Lovely weather,' said the postman, as he drew up outside the cottage in his little red van.

'Lovely weather,' said the man at the garage, as he filled up the car with petrol.

Lovely weather, lovely weather . . .

Not for us.

'Damn the sun,' I would murmur repeatedly during the course of the day. 'Damn the sun.'

The sun is no friend to the early daffodil grower. A mild, sunny March morning, everyone rejoicing that winter seems to be over, birds singing, romance in the air . . . and the daffodil grower is frustrated.

'Don't go on so,' said Jeannie, cheerfully, on this particular morning. I saw her point. I had already damned the sun five times.

'It maddens me, though. It's warmer than the summer.'

'But you can't do anything about it.'

Missed opportunities are what one regrets as one grows older; opportunities missed by a momentary lack of boldness, or a fear of hurting someone's feelings, or because, when the opportunity came, one was blind to its value.

I went up the lane, dumped the dustbin in its usual place, turned the car and drove back. It is a narrow lane with a ditch alongside much of its length. In summer, when each side is dense with such wild flowers as old maid's lace and clumps of pink campion, it is even narrower. Although, in due course, I cut these sides down, I postpone the task for as long as possible. One reason is that the lane is so beautiful in its wild state, and another is that it provides fledglings a place in which to hide during those first few days after leaving the nest.

Nonetheless, the lane causes problems for some drivers. An American couple from San Francisco once appeared apologetically at the cottage door with news that their car was wedged in the ditch. And another time, a young man arrived to tell us that his van was at right angles in the ditch near Monty's Leap, that he had driven from London and that his mother was a cripple and could not get out. Both situations were dealt with successfully. The Americans showered us with chocolates and the son and the mother have kept in touch with us ever since.

I envy placid people. I envy those who appear to lead normal lives, to have normal relationships, normal emotions. The complications of life which pursue the rest of us do not seem to affect them. They do not seem to suffer from imaginary fears or financial worries or contradictory secret thoughts. If you go into their homes, you find the rooms are tidy, the furnishings apparently new, fresh paint on the woodwork, and not a speck of dust to be seen. Their homes are as well organised as their minds. Everything is under control. There is never a reason for them to wake up in the early hours of the morning and worry.

I have always been a worrier. I have spent months of my life worrying in the early hours of the morning because I have never been able to take happiness for granted. Happiness, in my imagination, should be like a calm lake without a ripple upon it; and no prospect of a ripple. Unfortunately, although there have been many times that I have seen this calm lake, my imagination has also seen the ripples that might come. So I am, from time to time, pestered by unnecessary worries. I have worried often that I have talked too much at a party, and said things which I did not really mean. I worry, of course, about world conditions, but that particular worry is universal. I worry about the green-houses and their condition. I worry, in moments of hypochondria, about myself. I worry about the memories of long-ago meetings, which remain so fresh in my mind that I can vision the occasion and, in retrospect, be aware that the cause of their failure was my fault. I worry about anything in my small world, if I am in the mood.

Margaret, our friend from the pottery and our help during the daffodil season, arrived at the cottage with a beautiful greeny-brown jug which Jeannie had ordered from her. The two of them gossiped for a while and then, as Margaret was leaving, Jeannie happened to say, looking across the moorland on the other side of the valley:

'Isn't the bracken lovely with the sun on it? Every day of our lives Derek and I say how lucky we are to gaze on the land. In our minds we call it our own.'

There was a pause. Margaret was silent. Then she said, 'Didn't you know it is about to be sold? Didn't you see the planning application in last week's *Cornishman*?'

'Let's go to the bridge,' I said to Jeannie, as we watched Margaret's car disappear up the lane. 'There's no place better to talk about this shattering news.'

We walked up the path and turned left by the escallonia, and stood there looking across at the land on the other side of the valley. From that moment when we first came to Minack, the land we looked out upon had been a part of ourselves.

'Strange, isn't it?' said Jeannie, 'what the couple said to us this morning.'

The couple came every year to see us. They had followed the *Minack Chronicles* since their beginning.

'Yes,' I said, remembering how they had stood just where we were now standing, looking across the moorland and the sweep of Mount's Bay. One of them said, as if it meant as much to them as to ourselves, 'You must always keep this view!'

'And now it may go.'

'Darling,' I said, my serious crisis calmness taking charge, 'we must collect the facts. First, let's find the *Cornishman* and find out about this planning application.'

The planning application requested permission for a caravan, water supplies, and a cesspit in the corner of the field within thirty yards of Monty's Leap.

'They don't understand,' said Jeannie, 'what that land *means* to us. It is our whole life. Maybe that is being sentimental, but it's true. Other people buy property just because it is property. We're wanting to buy that land because it represents to us a kind of magic. We're not being sensible in that we are thinking of it as an investment or that sort of thing. We are wanting to buy the view, buy the safety of not seeing another part of Cornwall being rationalised. It is a dream we are wanting to buy.'

It so happened that Ron Messum, our accountant, arrived at the cottage on the very morning that I had been told of the price of the land. I led him indoors, and he sat down on the sofa which had been a part of so many crucial stages of my life, and I proceeded to tell him the full story, from the moment we had heard the land was for sale to this present moment when we had decided to make an offer.

His reaction startled me.

'Make an offer?' he said. 'Crazy thing to do!'

'Why?' I said.

'Don't you realise you'll start an auction? You've got two people for sure who are rivalling you. You've been asked for a firm price . . . but, if you start bargaining, the estate agent will go back to the others and the auction will start. And from what you tell me, they've got the money . . . and before you know where you are the price will go right out of your reach. So, just in order to try saving a few hundred, you will lose the land.'

He paused.

'Now,' he said, and he was fumbling in his pocket, 'here's 10p . . . go at once to the nearest telephone kiosk and tell your solicitor that you accept the price.'

'What about getting the money for it?'

'Don't worry about that now. The bank will lend it to you . . . but you get the land first.'

I obeyed him.

Incidents like this are so trivial against the background of world events. Yet it is the collection of trivial incidents that help to create the fabric of our lives. Without them our lives would be barren. Often we may be mesmerised by great events, great theories, great indignations, but frequently these are inspired by a kind of mass hysteria. In such situations, we do not belong to ourselves; we belong to a manipulated herd. We become insensitive to the trivial incidents, sad or happy, superficial or deep, which fill our lives with meaning.

'Sometimes I wonder, Jeannie,' I said, 'how we have done what we have done in our lives. Neither of us has a brain which is equipped to delve into detail.'

'I think we have common sense,' she said, 'and I think we both have intuition.'

My mind went back to a famous politician, Viscount Swinton. He was Secretary of State for Air before World War Two and it was he who was the driving force behind the development of radar, and who organised the factory production of the Spitfire in time for the Battle of Britain. He took interest in my career, befriended me by recommending me to influential people, and I remember that he once said to me: 'Men may have great power, have great knowledge . . . but if they do not possess the antennae of intuition they have nothing.'

I took out the Condor before breakfast on Michaelmas Day, the day we became landowners.

The Condor is a formidable machine; a monster rotary cutter, and I career with it over the bulb meadows in late summer, cutting down the grass. Many of the meadows, however, are covered by high bracken, and then I plunge the machine through the bracken, pulverising it.

'Stay here,' I suggested to Jeannie, 'while I make the path. You can watch me through the bedroom window.'

The eighteen acres, except for the two fields, were mostly covered by bracken, jungle-high bracken, and my purpose was to cut a path through it so that, after breakfast, we could take a celebration walk.

'I was remembering the fire which swept through all that land,' said Jeannie, 'and it left everything a charred mess . . . yet by the spring the bluebells were blooming again and we walked across to Carn Barges, Monty following us. Doesn't seem all that time ago.'

'Even then, we were wanting to own it.'

'Where are you going to cut the path?' Jeannie asked.

'I don't really know. I'll just have to find my way.'

'Make it a token celebration path. Don't try to do too much,'

I did not go far, bearing in mind what Jeannie had said, in making the celebration path. I was driving the Condor blind, but this was not as blind as I make it appear. For I knew there was a track where I was making the path, just as I knew there were other tracks, now hidden by bracken and undergrowth, on the rest of the eighteen acres. It was just a question of finding them; just as it was a question of finding the track for the celebration path. I was making good progress when I was suddenly faced by a hump of granite rock and, when I swerved to avoid it, the blades of the Condor crashed into another hazard, a collection of dislodged hedge stones. For a moment, until I switched off the engine, there was the horrendous clatter of the blades against the stones. At this point, therefore, I decided the celebration path had been completed. There would be time enough to continue the path round the land and, in due course, make other paths.

So I returned to the cottage, and to breakfast.

'What are we going to call this land,' said Jeannie. 'We must have a name for it.'

'This is your province, isn't it?'

A gentle joke.

'Well, I know what I would like to call it.'

'And what's that?'

'I think it ought to be called Oliver land . . . after all, we saw him there first and, if it hadn't been for him, there wouldn't have been an Ambrose.'

We had, by now, reached the gate that opened into the clover field and I had untied the string which connected the gate to the gatepost when, behind me, came the sound of a miniature yap and this was followed by rapturous noises from Jeannie. Ambrose.

'*What* are you doing here?' asked Jeannie, bending down. '*Where* have you been?'

I shuffled by the gate. This was Jeannie in the full flight of cat language, and I had planned a quiet walk on the celebration path. Ambrose was going to hold us up. Ambrose was going to spoil the occasion.

'Leave him,' I said irritably. 'I want to show you what I've done. Leave the cat alone.'

'Leave the cat alone? What did I hear you say?'

'This is special . . . I don't want to miss it. The moment, I mean.'

Jeannie, sensing that my dormant anti-cat attitude was rising to the surface, responded.

'He doesn't want you,' she said, speaking down to Ambrose. 'You'll have to stay here.'

But he did not stay.

He followed us. I had never known him to follow us so far from the cottage. He even stopped halfway up the clover field and made his mark, proclaiming to every other wandering cat that they were on Ambrose territory.

He followed us to the right, towards the badger sett. He was trotting behind us confidently. There was no doubtful miaow. He sniffed at a badger hole, then another, and my mind went back to an occasion when Lama went down a badger hole, and we spent hours and hours persuading her to come out.

Ambrose passed the badger sett.

Then we were walking the true celebration path, the path where the Condor had pulverised the bracken, until we came to a sudden stop at the hump of granite rock which had been hidden in the head-high bracken.

Ambrose, too, came to a stop at the rock. He jumped up on it and, without hesitation, began to purr.

We sat on the rock for a while, feet dangling. Ambrose between us, purring. A granite slab of rock, aeons old.

'An Everest moment,' said Jeannie.

Jeannie's definition of an Everest moment is when a long-awaited occasion totally measures up to expectation.

'Do you know what I'm going to call this rock?' went on Jeannie.

Another name for her to invent.

'What is it to be?' I asked.

'The Ambrose Rock.'

'An Everest moment . . . the Ambrose Rock. Yes, I see the connection.'

'I'll never for the rest of my life forget this moment,' Jeannie said, 'and I'll come and touch the Ambrose Rock and relive it.'

'You're a romantic.'

'You know I am . . . like you.'

I stood there on the bridge, happy that I was back in a world of uncontrived pleasures where the senses come into their own. So much knowledge is pumped into us that imagination becomes dulled. We are filled with information and expert opinions, and rules based on theory supersede instinct based on experience in the making of decisions. We reach the stage when we look, but do not feel. We live along the surface of life, then wonder why inner satisfaction eludes us.

Of course, there are those who will say it is nonsensical to romanticise the simple pleasures in times of great economic distress. We have, however, always been in periods of great economic distress. Generations have been promised the Utopia which is never reached, and yet there is this pressure put upon us by elitist groups to make us feel foolish if we enjoy uncontrived pleasures. Such people seem to think it is better to knock than to build; to destroy confidence in established standards; to exploit the sordid rather than the virtues, and often to create controversies regardless of the truth. In the struggle for notoriety and financial survival, they daily search for sensation at the expense of integrity. Perhaps they are the necessary ingredients of progress, and this I can understand. I refuse, however, to believe that they contribute to the happiness of those who are seeking peace of mind within themselves.

Dreamers may walk our land; those, young or old, whose worries can be stilled by solitude amongst wild beauty; who can become refreshed by the sense of time-lessness, and so free themselves for a while from the complexities of the struggle for personal survival. These complexities seem to me to become ever more compli-cated when I read and listen to those who pour out words of advice, religious or political, about solving them. I become bewildered, as if lost in a dense verbal forest. I admire the skill of the speakers and writers who can produce such verbosity, and they may create an image that they are leading their followers to a nirvana, but to me they are only leading them to further con-fusion. Simplicity, I believe, is what one should seek. Bury the myriad theoretical dogmas which have brought such distress in the past, and strive to achieve simplicity in behaviour towards others, in one's thoughts, in one's daily life.

'The test of religion, the final test of religion, is not religiousness, but Love.'

I recognise the dreamers because they are the vulnerable ones. They come within the category of the insecure, those whom personnel managers describe as non-executive material. They are those who have romantic fantasies and expectations. They are those who will understand without you laboriously having to explain. They are those who, at some moment of their lives, may have failed to accept an opportunity which awaited them, or have been saddened by a hoped-for relationship which did not materialise. They are the sensitive. I am at ease with the dreamers. They are seekers of simplicity. They are at home amongst wild beauty because they find solitude a solace; a moment for peace of mind.

A moment, now and then, is all one can expect. Peace of mind can never be permanent. There is always, in the wings, failure, or anger, or frustration, or financial worry, jostling to destroy it. The peace of mind that I know comes from those moments when suddenly, exultantly, I become aware of the magic around me, aware of mysteries that man-made devices can never explain. I feel free of being a computer number. I am alone with myself. I am part of the magic.

A Quiet Year

Weeds seem to me to provoke a form of horticultural class warfare. Weeds are belowstairs, flowers are above-stairs. I have often wondered how it was decided what should be flowers, and what should be weeds; and why it should be that, unlike the manmade social scene, weeds have never been able to edge their way upwards in the garden social scene.

'Valentine's Day, and the post has come. There are no Valentine cards for either of us . . . but there is one for Ambrose!'

Ambrose our cat.

'Let me see it.'

It was warm in the porch where we were sitting, a sunny morning, a summer-like morning. Above us was Knocker the gull, squashing his webbed feet against the glass. Knocker who maddens us sometimes as he bangs the glass with his beak, demanding attention.

Jeannie looked at the card, though it was not a card in the sense of a shop-purchased card. It had been drawn by the sender. A large heart on one side, and on the other side two cats sitting on a wall . . . one of them a coquettish lady ogling a stern gentleman cat; and a wispy line above the lady cat led to the message: 'You are the one for me!'

'I know who inspired that,' said Jeannie, 'Lovely Boy!' Lovely Boy was a Seal Point Siamese who lived in a Mayfair flat where he was doted upon by a very old friend, Eric Hiscock, doyen of the London book world. Eric had known me since my anti-cat days and had watched me change my attitude. First Monty, then Lama, then Oliver and Ambrose.

'We must frame it,' said Jeannie. 'I've never known a cat receive a Valentine card before.'

'I've only received one in my life myself,' I said, 'and I never discovered who sent it.'

Jeannie was sitting opposite me, the small oblong table between us, her back to the glass side of the porch which looks out on the tiny garden. She was wearing a white Arran-style sweater of cable and other complicated stitching that a friend had specially knitted for her. With her dark hair, white always suited her.

'I've had three, I think,' she said, 'and I never knew who sent them either. I used to look at my boyfriends and wonder. I'm not sure that I liked having them. I felt I had been put at a disadvantage.'

'Valentines can be a joke or a secret weapon,' I said. 'I remember sending one to a girl whom I thought I loved but who didn't care for me . . . and I had pleasure in thinking that at last I had aroused her interest, though anonymously.'

'Subtle of you, but not very kind.'

'It didn't do any harm.'

'I dreamt last night I was young again,' I said inconsequently as we walked up the lane towards the gate which opened into Oliver land.

'Do you remember if you were glad?'

I sensed Jeannie was amused, as if I had made a funny joke.

'I woke up feeling uneasy.'

The day was very still and the sounds we heard belonged to stillness: the mew of a buzzard high in the sky, a magpie chattering, a sudden brief song of a robin, the throb of a fishing boat on her way to Newlyn, the sound of our feet on the lane. There was the sweet knowledge of privacy as we walked; at that hour of the morning and at that time of year no one was likely suddenly to appear. There are those who shun privacy, preferring the noise and activity of the herd. Others value privacy beyond price. Privacy not of the hermit, but that of freedom from the raucous.

'Why uneasy?'

'I lived within a framework of permanence and permanence doesn't exist today. I am thinking of permanent values, permanent standards. One wasn't clouded as to what was right or wrong. It was simpler to control the route of one's life.'

'Do you really mean that? There was the war, and before it broke out always the shadow of war.'

'There's that shadow today. At this very moment someone could press a few buttons and every city in the country could be destroyed . . . I leave war out of my reasoning. I am talking about the fabric of life as my youth knew it compared with what it is today. In the practical sense, we could walk city streets at night without fear, or go to football matches without fights breaking out around us. In the spiritual sense, we relied upon our imaginations. We read books, shut our eyes, and imagined we were living the story ourselves. We were not tempted night after night to stare at a small screen, staring thoughtlessly. We were not victims of the hype.'

There have been many profusions of purrs since the first time Ambrose jumped on to his rock: on March days when the adjacent curved meadow is yellow with daffodils; on May days when bluebells touch the air with their soft scent; on summer days when foxgloves peer into the sky; and on winter days when the bracken is brown and flattened. The Ambrose Rock has become a talisman for us. Indeed we sometimes treat it as if it was a wishing-well. We touch it and wish, as if we believe there is a link between ourselves and the timeless watchfulness of the rock which gives it a secret power.

Jeannie, however, has always been in the habit of making wishes. When there is a new moon, for instance, a sliver of light in the night sky, she will perform strange antics, bowing three times to the new moon, turning round three times, blowing a kiss three times, each time secretly making her wish.

When we began, amateurs could earn a living from a flower farm in the area where we lived. True, there was the occasional devastation by gale, very occasionally by frost, but for most of the time the climate was on our side. Winters were warm and violets, anemones, Calendula flourished in the open ground; and the daffodils were ready to be sent to market long before those up-country were even showing through the soil. Cornish growers, therefore, were on their own in marketing flowers. No competition at that time from vast greenhouse hangars of forced daffodils. No competition from prairie-sized fields of daffodils, fields kept free of weeds by chemical sprays. The flowers we grew were as nature intended them to grow.

It was a period when parish worlds were stable and the lives of villagers were governed by the seasons. A horse or two could still be seen pulling a plough, wages did not automatically rise each year, a pound spent in a pub meant a thick head in the morning, unemployment was five hundred thousand, a dark face a rarity, hedges were cut by a sickle, bracken-covered meadows by a Father-Time scythe. There was a sense of permanence: steady jobs would always be steady, values maintained, the moon was safe from Man, great industries would always be great industries. Television had not reached into every home, extolling violence, creating envy. The silicon chip was still a dream in the inventor's mind. Life was safe for those who wanted to play it safe. Opportunities awaited those who were ready to take a risk.

One of Harrods' buyers had seen in Covent Garden daffodils we had been sending called, in Cornwall, Obvallaris, the botanical name of a daffodil first discovered growing wild in Wales at the end of the last century called Tenby. Such a lovely little daffodil, like a miniature King Alfred, and it has always surprised me that the large professional growers ignore it. Perhaps it is because it has an unreliable flowering record; a year, two years may go by and there is hardly a bloom to be seen. Then a year will come when there is a profusion.

There was a profusion this year when Harrods, through our Covent Garden wholesaler, gave an order for fifty dozen bunches towards the decoration of the main hall during a British Week. All the fashionable daffodils were available for Harrods: daffodils with high-sounding names like Golden Ducat and Unsurpassable and Golden Harvest, yet they had chosen our humble Obvallaris.

Those who saw them in the main hall, overheated, overcrowded, a humming noise of conversation, could not have been expected to imagine from whence they came. They could not have imagined they had come from meadows overlooking the sea of Mount's Bay; meadows bounded by blue elvan rocks and thick hedges of blackthorn; meadows with trowel-shaped holes where a badger had been digging for a bluebell bulb;

meadows where, if you are picking in the early morning, you catch the scent of a fox as you bend; meadows poised over a turbulent sea where a gannet might be diving unafraid; meadows so sheltered by ancient stone hedges and rock formations that you can stand there untouched by the wind or by a gale which roars at you when you leave the peace of the cliff. In such meadows we picked the Obvallaris for Harrods ... natural daffodils of the cliffs which had been growing there for decade upon decade.

A sad wonder of cat life is that cats have no road sense. So intelligent, so alert to the gentlest of noises, so able to look after their personal welfare, yet they have no awareness of speed. Every hour of the day there is somewhere a cat, a confident cat, a cat busy on some personal mission, a cat with a loving and comfortable home, a cat who is blind to the dangers of the road.

I have heard the story too often, shared in my mind the agony of loss, and then been grateful for the warning it has given me. It is easy to become complacent about everyday living, allowing habit to dull the sense of watchfulness – a hasty run down a path resulting in a fall, a careless use of a familiar tool, unnecessary haste in a car when nearing home – and so one can be grateful if somebody else's misfortune wakes one up from complacency.

There I was one morning, sitting on one of my seats which we jokingly called the Intime because it is so small that two people must sit very close together, and I found myself thinking how much of my life had been spent looking for Svengalis.

When a boy, my mind seemed to be in a prison and I searched desperately for someone to open the cell door. I wanted someone to awaken my dormant desire to study literature, tell me which books I should read and what I should look for in them. This, in retrospect, sounds such a simple ambition, easily achieved, and the more so since I was being expensively educated at Harrow. Yet there was an invisible barrier between me and anyone who could have helped me, and I found no master who saw me as a boy who craved enlightenment.

It was my shyness, however, which let me down when I was with my father. He and I shared an enthusiasm for trout fishing and we would go off together to the Fowey River near Bodmin Road station. Having parked the car and put on our waterproof leggings, we would walk to the nearby wood store and pass through the gate to the river. There we would set up our rods and tackle and select a fly which seemed suitable for the day and time of the year, and then begin to cast our lines. I was a schoolboy but already I preferred to be a solitary person. So did my father. We would fish a quarter of a mile apart.

It was the car journey to the Fowey River which provided the opportunity to talk. But we only chatted, and that was all. Yet my father would suddenly show his affection for me by putting a hand on my knee as he drove, murmuring: 'Dear Cur.' The word 'Cur' was one of those incomprehensible family endearments which were a cover for the middle class who, while wishing to show affection, yet felt embarrassed by so doing. 'Cur' was indeterminate. The name Derek was too definitive.

I always knew that my father was on my side and every now and then he would bestow on me a snatch of wisdom which was to live with me always. For instance, one evening I was with him on a Cornish cliff marvelling at a sunset, and I began to analyse the colours. He broke in and stopped me.

'Enjoy the sunset,' he said, 'don't analyse it. Too much analysing destroys the pleasure of magic.'

I left the seat we call Intime where I had been ruminating and began slowly to walk round the most faraway part of Oliver land. The grass path was barely a foot wide, bluebells crowding either side, and the tiny flowers of the stitchwort were scattered among them. Infant bracken was beginning to show, their fronds curled, resembling a baby's fist. Gorse, their cushions of golden petals hiding the spiky leaves, at intervals wafted their scent. A lark was singing above the fields inland to my left and to my right among the scrubland a whitethroat burst into a frenzied chattering. I looked for it and saw it perched on a bramble, and I marvelled that this tiny bird, which a few weeks before was in North Africa, had now taken up its summer home on a Cornish cliff.

It is an incident like that which makes me want to worship not God but Creation. God may be a symbol for mankind to worship but mankind, it seems to me, has misused the symbol. Mankind expects too much of

God. It is absurd, for instance, for two opposing sides to pray to God for their success.

Mankind has also, I believe, misused the symbol of God by involving God in politics, by exciting competition among different religions, producing animosity as a result, so that instead of love there is hate, instead of peace there is war. How many religious wars have there been in history? How many are in progress today? God, it seems to me, is used as an alibi by those who wish to legitimise their ambitions.

God should be freed from being used by mankind; and instead there should be worship of Creation. Creation is anything that moves, anything that scents, anything that is magical, anything that logic cannot explain, anything as ethereal as courage and kindness; and it is anything that inspires music, art, beauty. Creation can be worshipped without anyone meddling. Creation is what God was in the beginning.

On early summer mornings the scent of dew-touched honeysuckle breathes across our land, reminding me of the *Tiare Tahiti*, the flower of the South Seas. The flower that girls of Tahiti used to garland their lovers and now garlanded tourists.

I was there during the years before the Hitler war, lured there because it was a romantic world loved by Gauguin, Somerset Maugham, Robert Keable and Rupert Brooke, and all who sought tranquillity and happiness away from the conventions of western civilisation.

I have a tangible memento of my time there: a *pareu*.

A *pareu* is about five feet long and three feet wide and the cloth of mine has variegated patterns in red and yellow. I had many uses for it in the South Seas. Sometimes I used it as a carrier bag, wrapping my belongings in it, tying it on the handlebars of my bicycle when I pedalled round Tahiti or Moorea. Sometimes I used it as a sheet to cover me on hot steamy nights and often I used it as a towel after a swim in a lagoon.

The main purpose, of course, is to wear it, either by wrapping it round your middle like a bath towel, or in the more complicated way of the local inhabitants. This latter way can cause predicaments unless tied correctly. I had such a predicament one night when I was dancing energetically at a birthday party where I was the only European present. I was staying at the time in a *faré* built on bamboo sticks at Papeari at the far end of Tahiti, and my host was a fat happy old Tahitian called Mauu, a legendary figure in the islands, who had known my heroes like Gauguin and Rupert Brooke. There I was dancing when my *pareu* slipped. Everyone roared with laughter and Mauu called out in Tahitian, and by this time I spoke the language: 'You're in good company: Rupert Brooke was the same, he could never keep his *pareu* up either!'

It was an eerie moment in my life: a guitar playing, dancers stamping their feet, a lilting sound of singing, water lapping bamboo stilts, a moon shining above the Presqu' Isle de Tahiti ... and suddenly I was linked with a man who wrote:

> *Manua, when our laughter ends,*
> *And hearts and bodies, brown as white,*

Are dust about the doors of friends
Or scent a-blowing down the night,
Then oh! then, the wise agree,
Comes our immortality.

Lines too simple for many, but from a schoolboy they had captured me . . . a poignant cry about transient love.

Jeannie, when I was in the South Seas, had also found her version of a South Sea Island which was to influence her always. Pinchaford was the name, an old farmhouse on the edge of Dartmoor where she remembers sun-drenched holidays, uninhibited happiness, early-morning gallops across the bracken-covered moors, lazing by the swimming pool, laughing with young men who were soon to die in the war.

Pinchaford was her South Sea Island. She too, unsuspectingly, was on her way to Minack.

Down the lane in his car came our friend Leslie Payne, who was then the local postmaster at St Buryan. It was part of the charm of Leslie that when he delivered a telegram he would hint at its contents before we had time to open the envelope. Thus, if it was sad news he would say, as he handed the telegram: 'Sorry about this,' or if it was good news he would say brightly: 'This will be a happy day for you!'

'*Bertioni's Hotel* splendid,' said the telegram. 'Letter and offer following.'

Charmingly, Margaret and Joan, our daffodil helpers, rushed to kiss Jeannie, while I, needing to get away with the daffodil boxes as quickly as possible, said to Jeannie we would celebrate on my return.

She was waiting for me in front of the cottage.

'What do you think I've been doing? I've been going round Oliver land, talking out loud, saying, "Oh gosh, oh gosh!"'

It was an unusual expression for Jeannie to use, and yet its simplicity mirrored her character. Jeannie was able to mix easily with people from any walk of life because success has never been a desire to satisfy vanity. She had achieved it unaffectedly. Yet there is an aspect of her which is significant: she is only at her best, in career terms, with top people. She understands their language. She is at a loss, however, when dealing with the unimaginative, and she becomes unsure of herself. But when she deals with top people she intuitively plays their game, to her advantage and theirs. It is as if she is playing on the centre court at Wimbledon.

This summertime, on days when the sun burnt down on Minack and the nights were warm, Ambrose changed his habits and developed a midsummer madness. He no longer slept on our bed, so leaving me free to turn when I wished to turn, and to stretch my legs and be spared my foolish concern that I might be upsetting him.

Instead, as dusk fell, he set out on a prowl around his private world. He had many enquiries to make, many places to visit. There was the hole, a mere crack between two rocks, through which a mouse escaped from him on the previous night. There was another hole in the corner of the stables where the bracken of donkey winter bedding was stored which, he believed, housed a family of mice. Such holes had to be watched.

These, however, were mundane adventures of the night, routine tasks. It was when he set off up the lane that the real excitement of the night began. There were, in the stillness, so many unexplained rustles in the undergrowth on either side. Was it a frog, or a mole, or a mouse, or a nibbling rabbit? He was in no hurry to find out. He was not hungry. He had had a plate of coley for supper. He could enjoy the luxury of prolonging his excitement. A curious rustle . . . and he could sit and watch and wait. He was like an angler on a riverbank.

At his leisure he would move away, and sometimes, after crossing Monty's Leap he would turn left into the greenhouse field, where the California daffodils grow, and where, wired in, is the kitchen garden. If he is in the mood he will jump up on the post which holds the hinges of the gate and proceed to patrol the kitchen garden. He performs on these occasions a valuable task, because mice proliferate, coming as they do from the adjacent wood, and they steal the pea seeds I have planted, and the lettuce seeds. Thus, in his role of a security officer, I welcome Ambrose's visits to the kitchen garden.

I often wonder how I would react if the cottage caught fire. A dramatic urgency forcing a quick decision. Which of the paintings would I first try to save? Surely Kanelba's portrait of Jeannie would be the first because it had been with us for all our married life, and before. But I would also have to seize Jeannie's own painting of Ambrose on his rock; and there were the exquisite John Miller pictures which we had collected over the years; and John Armstrong's; and that of the River Thames from a fourth-floor suite of the Savoy Hotel which Jeannie commissioned Julian Phipps to do for a Savoy Christmas card. There were others of Jeannie's own paintings: the cornfield spreading before the farmhouse at the top of the lane; Lama when we first saw her, hiding in the meadow where we grew marigolds; and Monty, painted on the last day of his life. All these pictures would have to be saved if I was suddenly faced with a fire emergency.

And what of the furniture, and the books, and the various china ornaments, and items like the first copy of Karsh's famous photograph of Churchill given to

Jeannie by Karsh himself before he even gave one to Churchill? That would have to be saved, so too another photograph of Churchill signed by himself, and also the compass which A. P. Herbert had at Gallipoli and which he kept on his famous Thames boat *The Water Gypsy*; and also the pottery cat which Howard Spring bought in Manchester to celebrate his first success, *Shabby Tiger*. All such items I would have to remember to save.

There was no autumn this year at Minack. Late summer turned into winter overnight when a westerly raged for forty-eight hours early in October.

I had gone for a walk along the coastal path across our land to Carn Barges in the late afternoon, and when I reached Carn Barges I sat on the corner of the plinth upon which the Carn stands, where Monty once sat, the edge of which was once smashed by over-keen members of a mining college who were seeking specimens of Cornish rocks.

I sat there, and the late afternoon was benign. A gentle sea, a clear sky except for a roll of billowy clouds far away in the direction of the Scillies. A skin diver's speedboat slid across the water like an insect. The dying sun caught the cabin window of a boat so that it blazed like a searchlight. A raven, high to my right, nagged a buzzard. I heard the distant croak of a pheasant and guessed it was on one of the paths I had cut with the Condor. Then to the east of Lamorna Cove I saw two of the fishing trawlers of Newlyn, grey, white foam around their bows, thrusting their way out of Mount's Bay towards distant fishing grounds. Then just beside me, spreadeagled in the sun on a lichen-covered rock, the brilliant red, white and black colours of a Red Admiral butterfly. It was not one that would migrate. Too late for that. It would hibernate in some corner of these Cornish cliffs or in a farm building.

Weeds seem to me to provoke a form of horticultural class warfare. Weeds are belowstairs, flowers are above-stairs. I have often wondered how it was decided what should be flowers, and what should be weeds; and why it should be that, unlike the manmade social scene, weeds have never been able to edge their way upwards in the garden social scene. Why should the yellow of a dandelion be considered belowstairs? Or a daisy which has chosen to appear on a lawn? Or what is wrong with the purple flower of a knapweed unless one has long been brainwashed into believing that one has committed a social error by not pulling it up?

When I set off with the brush cutter to the cliff mea-dows, I always suffered from being controlled by Pisces, my birth sign. I always argue with myself as to which of the meadows I should begin cutting. I will wake up in the morning and say to Jeannie that I am going to cut the far meadows, then change my mind after breakfast, saying I am going down Minack cliff, meaning I am going to cut the meadows which, with Tommy Williams, our eccentric, devoted, first helper, we first carved out of the untamed land that was to give us a livelihood. Once when he was pausing from digging up the potatoes, I saw him leaning on his long-handled Cornish shovel and heard him saying, as if to himself, as he stared out to sea: 'What more can a man want than a morning like this and a view like that?'

I move into a small meadow on a steep slope, the brush cutter slung across my shoulder, and begin weaving it to and fro like a scythe, the circular blade spinning at speed, the two-stroke engine roaring with a noise like that of a motorbike. I know every meadow so intimately that I will be aware that under one layer of bracken lies a clump of pink campion that flowers all through the winter, and so I will attack the bracken very delicately and save the pink campion. Violets also abound in these cliff meadows and I am always on the watch for them; and if by mistake I lop one off, I curse myself for doing so. I have to keep a look out, also, for an early primrose, and if I find a clump, I will switch off the brush cutter, lay it on the ground, then bend down to the clump and bury my face in the petals. When one is unobserved, one can behave at such moments in a very basic fashion.

We had just reached the cottage, hungry for breakfast, when the little red Post Office van arrived down the lane with our post.

Valentine's Day. Last year Ambrose had one. Jeannie and I had none.

This particular morning the postman delivered three letters. One was a bill. Of the other two, one was addressed to Jeannie, the other addressed to me.

'Jeannie,' I said, doubtfully, after opening mine, reading what it said, 'did you send this?'

She looked at me with amusement.

'Didn't you say last year that a Valentine card was a weapon of mystery?'

The Cherry Tree

*'I've learnt something about you today,' said Jeannie,
'that I didn't know before.'*

*'The secret of a happy marriage – the unexpected keeps
it alive,' I replied.*

A day lent, a day that comes between a period of
stormy weather, or of fog, or of drizzle, a day like this
first day of October when I was sitting on the white
seat, a few yards of grey chippings between me and the
cherry tree; a day of peace and sunshine and a blue sky,
a day when a break in the rhythm of one's life cannot
be imagined.

I had planted the cherry tree when my mother died. I planted other trees then as well, a red flowering hawthorn, for instance, close to Monty's Leap; and its red flowers hang in clusters on prickly branches over the edge of the little stream when May comes. At the bottom of our cliff I planted a solitary palm tree. This palm tree grew in one of the meadows where we pick our earliest commercial daffodils, its fronds sprouting like those of a palm tree in a South Sea island; and it became a landmark for mackerel fishermen and crabbers as they worked offshore in their little boats.

But the palm tree died on the night of the Mousehole lifeboat disaster. It was killed by the hurricane which raged from the south on that terrible night. The fronds were scattered by the wind. Some I found high up on the cliff, and only the trunk was left standing, gaunt.

Ambrose's life at this moment was as perfect as a cat's life could be. He was doted upon. He lived in an environment where no dogs could chase him; it was very quiet, no cars were likely to threaten him; he could come and go as he pleased, night or day; he had the winter hay of the donkeys to curl on in the Orlyt greenhouse close to the cottage; the bedroom window was always open at night for him to go in and out; and there was our bed on which he could sleep, pinioning my legs or Jeannie's legs if he so wished. He had no competition. He had a happy home, and the prospect of a continuing happy routine. Many people on this very day may wake up in the morning with a similar prospect, then are suddenly faced by a challenge they never expected.

Even a cat.

Hindsight judges a past situation intellectually because it has no means of recalling the emotions surrounding a past situation. Historians, for instance, in passing their judgement on a past event, are always at a disadvantage. They may have the facts, but they can never be aware of the emotions which created the facts. Similarly this applies to all of us when we reflect upon our past mistakes and missed opportunities. We may now condemn ourselves, but it was the mood, the now forgotten mood, that governed us at the time.

The fog came down again as we were having lunch, and, by the time we had finished, was clinging around the porch where we were sitting. I mentioned a photograph album at this point which contained photographs of my brother's previous visit; and Jeannie said she knew where it was, that it was in her studio, and it would not take a minute for her to fetch it.

She was away several minutes.

'What have you been doing?' asked my brother on her return. 'Feeding the birds?'

'Always doing that!'

I sensed, however, that she was in a state of excitement; and I could not understand why. Whatever the cause she was not going to disclose it in front of my brother.

I had to wait until we were alone.

'When I left you both,' she then told me, 'I went down the path feeling sad that the fog was thick again. Then I saw something which I could not believe was real.'

'What was it?'

'I saw a little black cat looking the double of Lama and Oliver . . . curled up on the grass at the foot of the cherry tree.'

Surrounding Jeannie's studio, which was several yards below where we were sitting, is a high stone wall, high enough to hide the studio from sight. It was on the top of this high wall that I first saw a little black head, then a thin little black body.

'That cat's back!' I called out loudly, loud enough to scare it and make it disappear.

There had been such excitement in the tone of my voice that Jeannie had jumped to the conclusion I was pleased to have seen it.

'A little black cat at Minack again! You are pleased, aren't you?'

'No,' I replied, recovering my composure, 'it's going to be a nuisance hovering around; and anyhow, where has it come from? It must have come from somewhere.'

What amazes me is how some people manage to be permanently tidy. Take them by surprise at any time of the day and you find their rooms as neat as if one of the Royals was expected. Nothing out of place, undented cushions, no spreadeagled newspapers, windows transparently clean, kitchen looking as if nothing had ever been cooked there, carpet as new; and if there is a porch, boots and mackintoshes are out of sight. I envy the gift of method such people possess. They are the doers, the organisers; and when something has to be done, there is no delay in the doing. They do not prevaricate like Jeannie and me. Cooking utensils are cleaned as soon as the meal is finished; personal debris on a desk is regularly removed so that there are empty spaces on the desk concerned. Where is the debris taken? It is a mystery to me – just as it is a mystery to me how anyone is able to keep a home tidy.

The metal detector was a new toy. I had had it a week and it had already provided me with a minor triumph. I found a silver knife which we had lost years before. I found it buried in a patch of ground opposite the stables. I was hovering the disc of the metal detector an inch above the patch when it suddenly emitted a banshee cry; and after a minute of digging in the soil with a trowel, I discovered the knife. Soon after I had another minor triumph. My metal detector discovered a purse and several copper coins of 1945 vintage.

'If you hold the trowel,' I said to Jeannie, 'I'll sweep the ground.' I was now interrupted by Fred and Merlin. They came thundering down the narrow path, Fred in the lead, and when they reached us they swerved to the right and into the entrance to the Brontë wood; and there they came to a full stop. I have a wire taut across the entrance. I had fixed it because the donkeys used to have a habit of entering the wood to gnaw at the bark of the trees. Thus they had to be banned from entering; and on this occasion they stood sulkily beside the wire, looking back at me and my metal detector, and Jeannie with the trowel in her hand.

I swept the grass-covered ground, swaying the disc of the detector to and fro . . . and there was silence. Then I looked up, and found the donkeys were watching me with fascination. What could he possibly be doing? I continued to sway. Then I looked towards the donkeys again, and saw that Fred, a very inquisitive-looking Fred, had begun slowly to advance towards me.

Jeannie at this moment said: 'Sweep over closer to me.'

I moved over.

I swayed the disc slowly.

There was a banshee cry!

'I've got something!' I shouted, as if a trout had taken my fly. 'There, Jeannie, just where I'm holding it. Go on, dig!'

The donkeys stampeded.

Heads up, Fred making a weird banshee cry himself, they fled up the path we had come down.

Cherry, so named because we found her at the foot of the cherry tree, was on the ledge of the stone wall between the apple tree and Jeannie's studio hut. I was relieved to see her. Her absence since the previous afternoon had made me impatient to see her again; and when

I saw her on this stone ledge, I picked up my field glasses and focused them on her.

The sun had come out, and I saw clearly a light-coloured line down her left side, as if fur had only recently begun to grow there.

And when Jeannie joined me, I gave her the field glasses, and asked her what she thought was the cause.

'This is extraordinary,' she said, after a moment of looking, 'it looks as if she's been spayed.'

Cherry, therefore, had belonged to somebody who had specially cared for her, somebody who must be pining for her at that very moment.

Where, where, had she come from?

It was now that Cherry truly began to be a part of our lives.

'I've learnt something about you today,' said Jeannie, 'that I didn't know before.'

'The secret of a happy marriage – the unexpected keeps it alive,' I replied.

Cherry, with her eye on us in the porch, quickly completed the first stage of her turnover gesture, and lay there wriggling, and displaying a feature of herself we had only partly observed before. From a distance, even from a few feet, she appeared to be all black, but now we were able to observe her in detail. There were flecks of ginger in her coat, and while two of her paws were jet black, a front one was cream with a narrow line of black in the centre, and a rear one had just a touch of cream. She had, too, a little shirt of cream but, as she lay wriggling, paws in the air as if she was kneading, it was her undercarriage that caused a cry of admiration from Jeannie. It was mostly black but a portion was the colour of apricot; when she repeated the turnover gesture a few days later I heard Jeannie call out: 'Come and look. Cherry is showing her apricots!'

Most of us are full of opposites. Jeannie, for instance, revelled in her time as publicity officer of the Savoy Hotel Group, and yet she equally revelled in isolating herself in a Cornish cottage.

She once received a telegram from the BBC asking her to appear on a late-night television programme in which she had to give her views on a television series based on Arnold Bennett's *Imperial Palace*. It was at the height of the daffodil season. One day she was bent double picking daffodils in the rain, and next she was being fêted in London; and she enjoyed both days. The truth is that emotional experiences are as unpredictable as a changing sea, and there are no rules to govern them.

Educational policy, however, aims to make people believe that such rules can be created through knowledge. No account is taken of intuition. Drench knowledge into the young is the policy; force them into the examination rat race and frighten them into believing that failure will deny them a happy future. Yet this cramming of knowledge can create a kind of straightjacket in the way one thinks. One tries to remember, in a crisis, what is in the rule book rather than relying on instant intuition. Art and literature are also often influenced by such a straightjacket. A promising artist may be so drilled into obeying the instructions of the art teacher that spontaneity is lost. Or a tutor, compelled by examination edict, will insist that a book should be studied with such clinical attention that any enjoyment of the book is banished.

A pity there are no Professors of Common Sense at universities. They might help balance this pursuit of knowledge. Common sense will have far more influence on the lives of the majority than knowledge crammed into their minds for the sake of examination results. Common sense is a constant companion. Common sense can often identify the base of a complicated problem which is denied to brilliant professional thinkers. Common sense can steer the future of failed schoolleavers. The possession of common sense is an asset which will always prevail.

I was sitting at my desk ruminating, and Jeannie was at the other end of the room, standing, her back to the log fire. She looked so young and pretty, slim in her grey slacks, her head and dark hair on the level of the lintel behind her.

I had been making notes of an idea for a few days, and they were in front of me on my desk.

'If Cherry is to stay permanently with us,' I now explained, 'I believe she ought to pass an examination, something which I will call "C Levels".'

'Poor Cherry, don't make it too hard for her.'

'What I have in mind,' I went on, 'is that if she doesn't pass the tests, we'll get rid of her.'

'Derek,' Jeannie said, sounding alarmed, 'you can't mean it!'

'Yes I do,' I said firmly. 'If she doesn't fit in with our way of living she's out.'

'You sound like a nineteenth-century headmaster, right out of *Tom Brown's Schooldays*,' Jeannie said. Then she added doubtfully: 'What are these C Levels she has to pass?'

I looked at my notes.

'There are nine C Levels,' I said.

'Nine? As many as that? Are you asking her to pass all of them? And what are they?'

'Out of the nine,' I said, and I sounded very serious, 'Cherry will have to pass five of them. That doesn't sound harsh, does it?'

'That depends on the C Levels. What are they?'

I proceeded to read them out. This was the list.

1. She must not catch birds.
2. She must be house clean.
3. She must not show interest in food on the dining-room table.
4. No rotovating of the carpet with her claws.
5. No digging-up of plants in the garden.
6. Must not be too friendly with strangers.
7. Must never wander far.
8. No bringing into the cottage of live mice or rabbits.
9. She must not cause us anxiety by hiding when she is called.

'There you are,' I said. 'These are her C Levels, and I

propose that we should judge the result on the anniversary of her coming here. If she passes she's here for good.'

Jeannie looked at me in astonishment.

'You're not serious ... The anniversary is nine months away!'

There is too much news. Past inhabitants of our cottage heard the news of Queen Anne's death, the American War of Independence, Queen Victoria's accession, without being cluttered by a multitude of subsidiary news. News that came to them was basic, never manufactured, never bearing the influence of political or commercial interests.

But today people are hypnotised by a well-groomed lady or gentleman staring at them while announcing a daily catalogue of woes. The pound is up, disaster for exports; the pound is down, disaster for imports. A picture comes on the screen of rows of Stock Exchange gentlemen frantically trying to obey the computers on their desks. Another picture appears of a bomb-blasted street in Northern Ireland. Another of violence in some African state. We stare back mindlessly at the announcer, watch the lips moving, then wait for the hovering smile which will accompany the inevitable closing item – a jokey item to counter the catalogue of woes.

Each morning I collected Fred and Merlin from the stable field where they had spent the night, and took them to Oliver land. This mid-April morning I found them at the far end of the field, grazing, and when I called them they took no notice; and so I left them there.

Then I stood in front of the cherry tree looking at the pink buds which were soon to burst, no leaves accompanying them, lichen decorating the branches instead; the grey-green curl of the bearded lichen which only grows in the purest air.

I was standing there thinking for no rational reason about friendship; and how delicate it is, first to gain it, then to nourish it. At first, when the promise of friendship seems to be there, you can so easily be shy of pursuing it for fear of being a bore. You know the possibility of this because you have suffered from such a pursuit yourself. Thus the alchemy which creates a friendship requires intuitive responses which respect no rational rule.

I was thinking also, on this particular morning, of the traps which threaten friendship. Never take sides in a quarrel; and in particular a quarrel between husband and wife. You can be sure that any word of comfort to one or the other will be used as a weapon; and so, having comforted one, you will have enraged the other.

I had walked to the Ambrose Rock, the donkeys accompanying me, and I was sitting there on the rock, looking back across the dip of the valley to the cottage. It was near the end of May. Around me was the scent of young bracken, and, bordering the path, white stitch-wort mingled with the bluebells. I could hear voices from the mackerel boats fishing offshore, and a cuckoo repeating its monotonous call from the direction of Carn Barges. There were other sounds: the harsh, excited trill of a whitethroat, the timeless song of a lark, a blackbird on the branch of a hawthorn proclaiming its love for the world; and there was the hum of bees. To my left along the path, edging it, were buttercups and numerous varieties of grasses; and there were the seeds of plantain resembling choirboys wearing white ruffs. Opposite me was a glaze of pink campion. Suddenly Fred approached me, then pawed the ground at my feet and pushed his head forward, and began licking my hand.

How uncanny it is that, as a schoolgirl on holiday, Jeannie used to pass our land when sailing in the *Scillonian* on the way to the islands. There was her future. There was the home she was going to love so passionately.

For me, since the beginning, it has been her courage which has meant our survival. I have never seen her in despair. I can fall into depths of depression, and moan about troubles real or imaginary, but Jeannie, when I have been in one of these moods, has never given a hint of surrender. It is not a bossy kind of courage, it is a very subtle one. It has been sustained by her intense joy in small pleasures. One day in the spring she walked on her own around Oliver land; and when she returned she rushed out these words to me: 'It was so beautiful there this morning, and I only wanted to *feel* the beauty. I just wanted to *feel* the white sprays of the blackthorn, the first bluebells, the celandines and the first buttercups. I just wanted to *feel* the courting of the birds, the clap of pigeon wings, the scent of the gorse, the deep pink campion. I was part of all this beauty around me. I *felt* that I was, I didn't think it.'

Then she added.

'How those pundits on TV last night would have despised me for speaking like this!'

The pundits, from the British movie world, had been airing their views as to why the British movie industry had declined, then showing clips from their recently-made movies which explained, not that they realised this, why the industry had declined. There was no feeling in them, no romance – just a superficial gloss.

'Another fourteen days,' said Jeannie one morning.

Fourteen days to 3 October, the anniversary of the day my brother Colin was with us, and Jeannie found Cherry curled at the foot of the cherry tree.

'She's done well, you have to admit it,' said Jeannie. 'Did you really believe when you drew up the C Levels that she would never catch a bird, or bring a live mouse into the cottage? She brought a live rabbit in, I know, but I rescued that.'

'There is still plenty of time for her to catch a bird,' I said, damping her.

Seven days, five days to go . . . People who had seen Cherry during the summer and knew about the C-Level deadline were writing to us, asking for news. We ourselves had been observing these visitors. Was it possible for one of them to have dumped Cherry near by to the cottage the previous summer, hoping that we would look after her, and now had come to find out if the plan had succeeded? But if she had been dumped, would she have been so thin when Jeannie found her? After a year she was plump and glossy; and the once finger-thick tail was a luxurious black plume.

Four days to go . . .

Three days . . . Walter Grose, Pied Piper of cats, came to tell us he was soon to have an operation on his eye. He had lost one eye many years ago, and the good one was fading.

'I was with a man the other day,' he said, 'who was grumbling about the foggy weather we've been having. "Don't you realise," I said to him, "you're lucky to have eyes to see it's foggy?" '

Two days . . . Oliver Hosking, wearing his customary beret, retired member of the longest established flower-growing family in Lamorna Valley, appeared. At that moment I was using my brush cutter to cut the grass in the orchard.

'Wish we'd had that kind of a machine when we had to cut acres of corn with a scythe,' he said. Then ruminating, 'Cutting corn with a scythe was governed by the wind direction, always had to keep the wind over the right shoulder, then by the correct strokes the cut corn was laid out in swathes.'

One day to go . . .

At midday a couple from Capetown came down the winding lane.

'We're going home next week, and we'll soon be seeing swallows flying around our house, for they begin arriving at the beginning of November. They might be Cornish swallows! Could you show us a swallow's nest?'

Although I gave them a welcome, I was aware I may have given the impression I had something else on my mind. I explained what it was, and as I began they looked at me anxiously.

'If a cat called Cherry,' I explained, 'doesn't catch a bird, or bring a live mouse or rabbit into the cottage between now and a quarter to two, a little over one and a half hours' time,' I had been looking at my watch, 'she will become forever a Minack cat.'

'Oh, what a relief,' the woman said, laughing, 'I thought it was something serious!'

The couple saw the nest in the garage, then left.

One hour, half an hour, ten minutes . . .

'Where's Cherry?'

'Cherry! Cherry!'

Ambrose, we knew, was asleep in the Orlyt.

'Cherry!'

Jeannie was holding the two saucers of chopped chicken. I was holding the bottle of champagne and the glasses.

'I will quickly give Ambrose his chicken,' said Jeannie. 'You go on calling for her.'

I walked down to the white seat, rested the champagne bottle and the two glasses against a rock, and went on calling for her.

She suddenly appeared, just as Jeannie came round the corner.

It was exactly a quarter to two.

'Cherry,' Jeannie said, 'you've done it! Here is a reward!'

Jeannie walked over to the cherry tree and placed the saucer at its base, the canopy of pear-shaped leaves above her; and in the same spot as when, a year ago, she first saw the frightened, skinny black cat.

Jeannie

'Only a bit of fantasy. I was asking what you would do if I were run over by a bus.'

'You know very well what I would do. I would stay here. I will stay here for ever and for ever, I will be here when I die, my spirit will be everywhere. I will love all those who live here and love Minack, but if any philistine misuses Minack, I'll turn into a witch and haunt them!'

Twelfth Night. The frolic is over, reality has taken its place.

Twelfth Night has always seemed to me to be a sad time, bringing apprehension.

'Aren't we lucky,' said Jeannie, 'to have each other?'

'Aren't we lucky?' was a phrase used often by Jeannie. It was a mirror of her personality. She never took happiness for granted.

Neither of us in all the years we have been together has ever doubted that we would always be together. Boredom is the menace in a marriage, not infidelity. We have had our rows, of course, and sometimes I have wondered whether we would have stayed together had we remained in London. Too much stress. Too many temptations. Too many late nights, tired days. But here at Minack there has never been any doubt: any row we might have has soon died away because of our isolation. No telephone with which one could fuel a row by talking to a sympathiser. We were a mile off the main road, and that blunted any prospect of fulfilling a threat like 'I'm leaving you!' Neither of us would relish carrying a suitcase that far.

'I've caught you in a web,' I would say to her sometimes, jokingly. 'I'll never let you escape.'

She did, however, escape occasionally, going to London on her own, coming back brimful of stories as to what had happened to her. The stories were always full of fun. She cascaded fun, and she effortlessly conveyed this sense of fun in whatever circle she moved.

Yet I have never felt that I have really *known* her, and that is because of the contradictions in her character; and she has never really *known* me because of the contraditions in mine. That is what made our companionship so exciting. We remained, in a way, strangers to each other. Every day was as if we had met for the first time. True, we belonged totally to each other, but we maintained our independence. We were like two islands joined together by a bridge.

Propinquity is the easiest route for a love affair. As the publicity officer of the Savoy Hotel, she knew all the people I wanted to know in my capacity as an MI5 officer responsible for reporting weekly to the Secretary of the Cabinet. My task, among many others, was to report the gossip and the mood of the influential people. I therefore began to see her often for practical reasons, making use of her in fact. Then, as my diary shows, she began to invade my thoughts, my desires; and she had a voice which bewitched me. I would ring her up and ask her to talk, talk about anything, just so I could listen to her voice.

She was one of the war generation of pretty girls who lived daily with death. Bombs on cities killed them. Lovers, temporary, permanent, casual, were every day reported missing. These girls had a role to play, providing a thrill, or offering a man in great danger an illusion of love, or acting as an anchor for the man to go back to, one leave after another; and long after one of the pretty girls had forgotten a man, he was remembering her. These pretty girls of Jeannie's generation were often confused. It was not easy for them to find the dividing line between having fun for themselves and consoling those who might soon be killed.

'Only a bit of fantasy. I was asking what you would do if I were run over by a bus.'

'You know very well what I would do. I would stay here. I will stay here for ever and for ever, I will be here when I die, my spirit will be everywhere. I will love all those who live here and love Minack, but if any philistine misuses Minack, I'll turn into a witch and haunt them!'

I have always felt when waiting for Jeannie, returning to Jeannie, a feeling of excitement. There has always been so much to talk about, personal, politics, literature, music, sport. Her interests were so wide that at one moment I might be arguing with her that I believed Hardy was a more profound poet than he was a novelist; next we might be sharing the view that the boring delivery tone of a BBC woman announcer made us turn off the news broadcast; next she might tell me of a visit to a one-time hairdresser during which he had asked her who was her favourite composer, and she had replied Puccini – 'Madam,' said the hairdresser, 'how brave of you to admit it.' Or we might talk of sport, any sport, and the ideas we each had would be tossed between us like a tennis ball in a tennis match. Or there would be solemn moments about politics. 'Why,' I remember Jeannie saying, 'are opposition politicians and the media so blind that they don't realise the Falklands War brought freedom to Argentina? Had it not been for Mrs

Thatcher and the Services the Junta would still be there, and the secret arrests would have continued.'

There was Auntie Mirrie's story of the Fairy Ring.

'We used to take Jean and Barbara for picnics in Welwyn Woods, and one day we were walking along chatting and laughing when Jeannie stopped dead, and whispered: "Hush! I see a Fairy Ring!"'

'We all gazed. There was a tree and just in front of it . . . a perfectly round circle of dark green grass. The other grass all around was the palest possible green. We were all astounded. I had never seen one before. Jeannie said that the fairies will be dancing on it tonight; and we crept very quietly away.'

Jeannie had told me this story. She told me it when, one summer's day years ago near a cove called Penberth, we were exploring the crevices, long disused tiny meadows, gloriously aware of the fun of life, scrambling up rocks, resting on one jutting out to sea, saying in our minds that we were in love, and we were on holiday, and one day we would live on this Cornish coast for ever, thinking of mad hopes because we were free, because we were far, far, away from sensible decisions, because we were intoxicated by the sense of antiquity which makes the passing fashions of mankind a laughing stock – there we were together when, suddenly, Jeannie said: 'Hush . . . look, over there beneath that rock, is a Fairy Ring!'

Not a ring of dark green grass this time. A ring of daisies. 'The fairies will be dancing there tonight,' said Jeannie, just as she had said when she was a child.

It was very hot those first two months at Minack, and it was like a furnace down the cliff as we dug our early potatoes. We often worked together on our own and, because the ambience of the beautiful scenery and its loneliness made us feel we were on a South Sea island, Jeannie would be naked as she picked up the potatoes while I, wearing boots, dug them up with my long-handled Cornish shovel.

Then after a while, Jeannie would suddenly say she had had enough and was going to have a bathe; and she would run away from me, down the foot-wide track to the rocks and the sea. I would watch her, this gazelle-like creature, and ponder how such a short while ago she was daily playing the role of a sophisticated hostess at the Savoy or the Berkeley or Claridge's.

She would pause at the point where the track fell steeply and took her out of sight. She would pause, and wave at me, her long dark hair falling over her bare shoulders. A few seconds later, gulls disturbed from their somnolent ruminating, rose from the rocks calling their weird cries; and telling me that Jeannie had arrived at the rock pool where she bathed.

We sat on a grass bank just above the rock where Lama sat when I took a photograph of her, the photograph that became the cover of my book *Lama*. Jeannie spread butter on a slice of bread, covered it with tongue and handed it to me; and as she did so a scene in the previous night's television news passed through my mind: a scene showing rows of madmen screaming into telephones, each with a miniature television screen in front of them. Screaming madmen of London, New York and Tokyo manipulating the world's money markets.

But for Jeannie and me we were sharing a halcyon moment of idleness that reached into our souls. No intellectual turmoil disturbing us into feeling guilty because we were happy. We were alone, together.

We were alone with an untarnished private world around us that stretched back unchanged through the centuries, placing modern mankind's madness into perspective.

'Jeannie,' I said.

'I'm here,' she said jokingly, a few inches away from me.

'I want you to concentrate.'

'I'll try. What about?'

'About next year.'

'Why next year?'

'I want it to be *your* year.'

'That sounds exciting, but what do you mean?'

'All this year, just as in other years you've cossetted me while I've been writing and doing all the other things I have been doing on the land. And when I've finished *The Cherry Tree*, but I don't expect to do this before November, you will be typing the manuscript, and then you'll be doing the illustrations . . .'

'I love helping you. I love doing these things for you.'

'But it's time to reverse the situation, for me to look after you.'

'Why?'

She was coaxing me to argue.

'Only that you have so much talent that you are not using.'

'I don't think I have.'

Then, she asked mischievously: 'How do you propose to organise the functional aspects of my year?'

'Oh please don't go into details.'

A gull had swooped down on a rock near us, hoping we had left over a piece of our breakfast. There was, as it happened, a piece of bread, and Jeannie threw it to him.

'But I'm interested,' Jeannie said. 'You must have thought this out. How, for instance, are you going to manage the cooking?'

She was teasing me.

'I'll do the cooking all right.'

'Do you really mean all this?'

'Of course.'

She put her hand into mine.

'It's going to be a wonderful year for me.'

We sat on the rickety seat in the honeysuckle meadow, Ambrose between us. We had strolled there before breakfast, the early morning sun warming us, and touching the honeysuckle, strengthening its scent. The meadow has an earth-filled stone hedge on one side, and it is guarded on the other side by a low, drystone wall. Around the rickety seat was a canopy of green leaves from an elder tree; and bushing along the drystone wall, facing the rickety seat, was the mass of honeysuckle.

If I had stood up and looked back, I would have seen

the cottage; and if I had been on the bridge above the cottage and looked across the valley, I would have seen the top of the elder tree, bare branches in winter, green in spring and summer. In front of us on that September morning, across the bracken-covered moorland, we looked upon the standing stone and the rugged cliff rocks of Carn Barges; and the sea.

'This is where I want to be when I die,' said Jeannie, 'left wild as it is now, untamed.'

'Me too.'

It was an appropriate place. Carn Barges, where we had stood, seeing the cottage for the first time, standing there in excitement, visioning our future. Carn Barges would be there to watch us when the story was over.

'Aren't we lucky?' said Jeannie, using her favourite phrase.

She was wearing her red coat, red, her lucky colour, on that day in September when she left for the hospital. It was a morning of thick mist, and while she was packing, I hurried, hidden in the mist, to the Ambrose Rock. I knew there were small pebbles in a crevice, and I collected one, and brought it back to Jeannie.

'For you to take with you,' I said, knowing she believed the Ambrose Rock was a magic rock.

When it was time to leave she first went up to the bridge, and blew kisses towards Carn Barges which she couldn't see because of the mist; and then to the Lama field behind where she was standing, and to the cottage. There was almost a gaiety about her, and she called out: 'I love Minack! I love Minack!'

I outwardly pretended meanwhile to be happy about Jeannie's progress. She was full of energy, typing away at my manuscript, losing no weight, her hair alive – and yet I was worried about her.

There was one evening in November when, after feeding the evening gull as dusk was falling, I walked down to the stables where Merlin was standing with his shaggy head in the doorway. It was a rough evening; the wind was coming from the south, and spattering rain had begun, and soon there would be a torrent.

'You'll be cosy here,' I said to Merlin when I reached him. Then I put an arm around his neck and began a monologue about my worries. I could never have spoken to a human being as I spoke to Merlin. There we were in the dying light of the day, the rain beginning to fall, the sound of the sea each minute becoming noisier as the wind raised its speed; and here was I feeling safe because I was alone with a donkey. No fear that anything I said would be passed on to another. No fear that I would be misunderstood. I stood there beside him, experiencing a depth of feeling that logic would never be able to accept. I had a spiritual glow as I pursued my monologue. I had a friend to listen to me that I could totally trust. When I was a child I had a similar friend, an Old English Sheepdog called Lance. He too listened to my monologues, and gave me comfort. I was safe with Lance. I was safe with Merlin.

In the middle of November she had another X-ray and check up. She had been suffering from a pain to the left side of her back, and we both were apprehensive when

I drove her to the hospital. She went inside, and I sat waiting for her to return, looking at my watch, hoping, waiting, waiting, and then suddenly I saw her running towards me (wearing her red coat), waving, and then I knew that all was well. Nothing serious had been found. The surgeon who had operated on her was delighted that she had put on 8lb in weight, and he told her he did not need to see her again until the middle of January. It was a euphoric drive back, and a beautiful moment when, half an hour later, I heard her cry out as we crossed Monty's Leap; 'Home! Home!'

17 January
She had an appointment with the surgeon today, and she wore her red coat again. I waited for her in the hospital car park . . . but this time when she reappeared she did not wave at me, nor run towards me.

'He didn't seem very pleased with me,' she said.

And we had a quiet journey home.

19 January
She did such a beautiful drawing of the cottage today. Only two more to do. She has such sparkle. She looks ageless. Her illness is an enigma. The X-ray yesterday showed up nothing abnormal. My own belief is that destiny is always in control, and so we just have to wait.

21 January
Illustrations of *The Cherry Tree* completed! They are wonderful, and I said to Jeannie that we must get them off straightaway, and I found out that British Rail have a service called Red Star which guarantees delivery over-

night. So we packed the illustrations up, and I took them to Penzance Station. So much effort, so much love went with them.

25 January

One of the most idyllic days of our lives. We were *so* close. We went to the honeysuckle meadow. It was eleven in the morning, the sun was shining, soft air full of sea scents, and a bee came flying around as we sat on the rickety seat, deceived into believing it was a spring morning.

'Oh, I'm so happy here,' Jeannie said.

Ambrose had come with us, and was sitting on the seat beside her, so I took a photograph of them both with my new toy, the polaroid.

'I suppose,' she went on, 'that we both have achieved all that we wanted to achieve when we were in our teens, dreaming about the future.'

'Not many can say that.'

'Neither of us have ever been greedy. I mean we have been thrilled by any success we have achieved, but our ultimate aim has always been to try to have peace of mind. If one is greedy, one never can have peace of mind.'

28 January

We passed Walter in the lane on our way to the hospital. Trigger and Whisky at his heels. I stopped for a moment, and he peered through the open window and said: 'You lucky man, having such a beautiful wife. Off for the day are you?'

2 February

St Michael's is a wonderful hospital, organised by nuns belonging to the Roman Catholic Order of the Daughters of the Cross of Liège.

'Everyone is so kind, so kind,' Jeannie keeps saying.

A nurse said to me: 'We are not supposed to have favourites but Jeannie *has* to be a favourite. She is always thinking of *us*.'

Jeannie's attitude towards the nursing profession was that *their* morale should be boosted just as much as the patients'. Nurses have to undergo such terrible emotional pressures and Jeannie believed that, whenever possible, patients should try to be cheerful.

9 February

It is Sunday. The streets were empty as I drove here, and now I am sitting answering letters by the window, and she is sleeping. A dog is barking, pause, it is barking again. Then the hideous electronic bell of an ice-cream van rings out. How I envy people who are insensitive to noise. The dog is barking again . . . how can there be a dog owner who will let a dog bark so senselessly on a peaceful Sunday afternoon, *and* near a hospital. The ice-cream van has rung its electronic bell again.

I went off to the hospital, and Jeannie was waiting for me with a bright smile – how dazzling that smile of hers has always been; and she proceeded to tell me how during the night she had woken, found it difficult to sleep, then in her mind began to visit Minack.

'I was lying on my side and knew I was facing

Minack,' she said, 'and every corner became alive for
me. You and I know what it has come to mean to
people, those who come to see it, finding their way
without any directions, and all those who have written
to us. I saw it all so clearly. Minack is a symbol, a kind
of anchor to those who lead stressful lives. People cling
to it in their minds, just as I was clinging to it as I lay
awake last night.'

While she had been speaking, an idea had come to
me, an idea which had to be put into effect immediately.
So I said to her, pretending, that I had run out of
toothpaste and I had to go into Hayle to get some.

'*Please* don't be long,' she said.

In fact I raced back to Penzance, to a firm of sign-
writers, and I explained to them what I wanted to be
done, had to be done within three days, cost did not
matter. It was of desperate importance.

Then I returned to Hayle and Jeannie, keeping secret
as to where I had been.

18 February
The sign was ready!

I didn't bother about the paper in which they offered
to wrap it up. I just took it, and raced off to Jeannie.
And when I reached her, to my joy, she seemed so
much better than the previous day, and I was able to
treasure her reaction to what I had brought her.

It was a two-foot-square wood sign with dark green
background: and in yellow on this sign were the words:

THE DEREK AND JEANNIE TANGYE
MINACK CHRONICLES
NATURE RESERVE

A PLACE FOR SOLITUDE.

'Oh Derek,' she said, 'oh Derek . . .'
Then she held the sign in her arms, and kissed it. I
left it there with her.

22 February
The sun was shining this morning. Daffodils were spattered either side of the winding lane. Carn Barges was
etched against the blue of Mount's Bay. The outline of
the Lizard was clearly to be seen.

A gull was on the roof.

A chaffinch expected a crushed biscuit up by the
bridge.

Ambrose and Cherry, side by side, no animosity
between them, waited for their breakfast.

Merlin was by the stable gate, hoping for carrots.

All seemed as it always had been, always would be.
Jeannie . . . and I remembered the words she had written
after Penny died:

> *The spirits of Minack*
> *Welcome you*
> *To their world of Forever*
> *Where life continues*
> *And death is never.*

The Evening Gull

I had the idea of her memorial service in the last day or two of her life. It was agony witnessing her brave, hopeful smile when there I was beside her thinking how she could be remembered.

My idea was not to have an ordinary memorial service. For Jeannie I had the idea that her memorial service on the chosen day could be held anywhere in the world, at any time, at any place convenient for anyone wishing to join in. Hence someone might be in a bus in London, or in an office in New York, or in a plane flying to New Zealand or Australia, or in a traffic jam in Toronto, or just locally in a field. The date I have chosen is 23 March, her birthday; and so I am sending out cards to those who write, and in due course I will put it in The Times *and the* Telegraph. *Here is what I am saying:*

Memorial Service for Jeannie

Those who knew Jean Nicol Tangye in her Savoy Hotel,

Claridge's and Berkeley world, and those who knew her as the heroine of the Minack Chronicles, are invited to join together in remembering her, sometime during Sunday 23 March, and wherever they may be . . . placing the Cornish daffodil meadows in their minds which she loved so much, as the setting of her Memorial Service.

*T*hree years since Jeannie's memorial service.

I wish I could believe in the philosophy that time heals. It depends, I suppose, on the depth of the wound that has to be healed. A shallow cut, and the healing is quick. A deep cut, and the scar remains. It is the same for all those who have lost someone they have loved. There will always be moments waiting to pounce, bringing back the pain, bringing back the vacuum.

I am lucky because I live in a world of natural beauty; and every blade of grass, every inch of soil, every ancient rock offers me the security of knowing that my roots are here, so giving me comfort. I am lucky also to have a motivation for my life. I will be fulfilling Jeannie's dream if I succeed in making watertight the future of Oliver land, and of Minack, safe from any philistine opportunist. The Minack Chronicle Trust is ready to take over if I were to be run over by a bus, but there are still imponderables to consider . . .

As for myself, my personal view of my future has always been a simple one. It is this. The only fear about death is the fear of what happens to the loved one, or the animals, who are left. 'Who will look after them?' is the worry.

Thus, if you die alone, without this fear, you die free.

Mike the postman was earlier than usual the following morning.

'A recorded letter for you to sign,' he said cheerfully.

I signed.

'Another lovely morning,' he said.

I opened the letter.

It was from the Department of the Environment Heritage Division.

Minack had been Listed. Minack was now a part of the English Heritage.